MW01493333

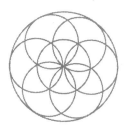

Advanced Praise

Rebirth *is a beautiful meditation on the multi-beings we all are, and why it can feel like a constant struggle to search for the self. It is a delightful, thought-provoking collection of stories and conversations, and I was deeply comforted and moved by it.*
–Annie Hartnett, author of *Unlikely Animals* and *Rabbit Cake*

It takes a particular eye to recognize Rebirth. *Kate's eye is fine tuned with wisdom, intelligence, sensitivity and humor. The stories within are true medicine, elixirs. They are real people leaving and arriving, listening deeply and taking the courageous steps to align the practical and the spiritual, inviting you toward a True North.*
–Ann Randolph, award-winning writer and performer

One after another, we are introduced to those who have manifested personal and professional success by birthing and sustaining a business and a life committed to living their purpose on the planet. Each story offers the reader a perspective that comes from Kate's witnessing and sharing the inspirational journeys of people who were not afraid to follow a dream.
–Noerena Abookire, Ph.D.

REAL-LIFE STORIES ABOUT
WHAT HAPPENS WHEN YOU
LET GO AND LET LIFE LEAD

REBIRTH

KATE BRENTON, ED.M.

INSPIREBYTES OMNI MEDIA

Rebirth: *Real-life Stories About What Happens When You Let Go and Let Life Lead*

Author's photo: Joe Longo

ISBN Paperback: 978-1-953445-26-1
ISBN E-Book: 978-1-953445-27-8
Library of Congress Control Number: 2022939027

 INSPIREBYTES OMNI MEDIA

Inspirebytes Omni Media LLC
PO Box 988
Wilmette, IL 60091

For more information, please visit www.inspirebytes.com.

For my mother, who birthed me

and

For my son, who rebirthed me

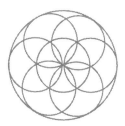

Table of Contents

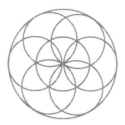

Introduction

How can Rebirth be a constant or a cyclical phase in our lives? Why do we want to welcome it, and how do we look for it when we are out of alignment? How does this mesh with finally *arriving* and enjoying life?

Let me tell you a story.

I grew up with true high-standing bangs fortified by the constant hairspray stream of the nineties. Let me catch you up: You curled the bangs up with a brush, high heat on the hair dryer, and spray, spray, sprayed until you created a simulated wave or claw. It was what you did. During these fashionable teenage years, my parents took to camping. Real-deal, old-school, walk-to-the-bathroom, sleep-in-a-tent camping, or antiquated cabins (which I personally abhorred) that you had to wear shoes to walk in. I hated it, publicly. I was also the oldest child (read, only teenager), and we would often take these trips with my two much younger siblings and family friends that also had younger children. From my teenage perspective, I dreaded these trips on multiple levels, and my family took ample time to remark on the fact that there would be no need for all that hairspray in the woods. We agreed to disagree.

Fast forward fifteen years, and I am dropping all unnatural products, leaning into vegetarianism, and opening up to the yogic arts. Honestly, there was an overlap of cheesesteaks and late Friday nights with yoga class and brunch on Sundays where the two me's were co-existing. One was a remnant of the hairspray (although the fashion had long gone, she was still interested in what the census of the public held as markers for who she was) while the other one was learning what mung bean soup was and rejecting (successfully) an early declaration of asthma by taking to running and yoga to overturn that label. I have lived through the time of transition from "what is no longer" to "what is becoming" several times over.

"How did the teenager that could not stand camping, up and move to Hawaii to camp on beaches and live in parts unknown? How did that happen to *you*?" my mom would joke on the phone when I called back home.

"I don't know," I would answer honestly.

I went from not being able to tolerate being dirty to having happy, red, dirt-stained feet. A Philly-born girl, primarily raised in the suburbs, found herself living at least two miles away from a street light.

However it happened (which is a story for another time), I grew to be more and more comfortable outdoors than indoors: living largely on decks and lanais, camping in hard-to-reach places, and learning how to commune with Nature in ways previously unconceived—by me or those that raised me, if I am honest. I became way more comfortable in elemental living and was able to mostly drop the burden of what I should or should not have, which is easy when your days are full of drinking fresh tangelo juice during citrus season, having more avocados than you can eat, walking your dog on the most gorgeous beaches, seeing the expanse of stars in the sky, drinking in fresh air, and learning that a whole other way of living and locus for abundance exists, and it is one that includes all things.

At one point, I was living at the base of my favorite mountain, and I only had three walls. My fourth wall was a screen. It wasn't luxurious. It was teeny tiny. My partner at the time used to laugh because he said you could see the bathroom from the kitchen—*into* the bathroom—because there was no door. But I loved it.

I woke each morning and heard the birds, felt the wind, and knew where my day was going. I sat on the front expanse and knew, in ways I didn't understand, that living this close to pristine nature with very light responsibilities because my needs were very light was a precious and fleeting gift. I'd learn later what the whisper meant.

When I would travel from that little mountain hut back to city life, I would joke that I could only be off-island for so long before my timer would go off. My skin would dehydrate, and I'd start to long for the mountains—I needed to go back. I would be traveling, working, and visiting with friends and family on each coast, and I'll tell you a secret: Even though they had air conditioning on, I would crack the window because I could not breathe. I had become so accustomed to fresh air that I could not breathe in a contained room because I felt so confined. That was a new thought. I didn't know walls could be confining. The *same* person that had hated camping now couldn't relax without an open connection to Nature.

And then I moved. I moved back to the depths and bustle of the city. It was really hard at first. It was even a bit depressing, but with a luxury of ample time, I scooted as far out into Nature as I could and enjoyed the dalliances of the city: great restaurants, new friends, new places to go and see. Eventually, it eroded; that finely tuned relationship to Nature dulled. The city-life expectations began to drown out the clamoring for a natural cadence. From a top floor apartment, my elemental relationship dropped away like an autumn leaf. Sure, I was outside more than others, and part of the connectivity stayed and found new ways to thrive, yet the raw and alive relationship of daily communion drifted further and further away.

Let's talk about the body for a moment. Your body and your Self can become accustomed to new things, and you can also adapt to things that are not, perhaps, in your best interest. From a body perspective, this means that when I was living more closely with nature, I had more energy, I was eating better, and I radiated more of that internal health that comes from the nourishment of fresh living. I correlate my internal changes with external shifts, but us humans can make lifestyle, mindset, and relationship choices that slowly turn us (or sometimes catapult us) a little further away from ourselves and our most thriving alignment—the one that makes us glow—no matter where we live.

I didn't stop to address how far I had truly turned away from everything that lit me up until one spring morning six years after moving back to my hometown of Philadelphia from a little Hawaiian island. Now a mother to a three-year-old son, I woke under my down comforter to realize I had become totally accustomed to closed windows, recycled air, and the luxurious supports that I thought were necessary to help land me into motherhood as I understood it. It simply was what was.

Is one way of living better than the other? I think that's a trick question now. I think it might be more about identifying where you are in the cycle of birth and rebirth, of growth and void. Whatever that ever-changing answer is, that morning as I watched the sun rise, I reached over and opened the window.

This book is an invitational window to the radiance of a new morning, both figurative and deeply literal. There is magic for you in the dawn, should you choose to meet it.

You can read this book cover to cover, or you can pop it open to whatever calls you. Each chapter stands on its own, sharing a story of someone rising up to change in their life, whether that change is welcomed or unexpected. Each story shares practical wisdom on the inevitable path of Rebirth.

Many of these interviews were recorded in 2020, when humanity was navigating an unprecedented rebirth. Each interview mentioned the difficulty and held the severity of this global, humanitarian experience. As a writer with the intention of sharing stories of awakening and upliftment, I did not necessarily include each person's reflection on this time, especially if their sentiment was mentioned in another chapter, as it could have disrupted the cadence of the work in its totality. Incidentally, some interviews happened before 2020. Although every effort was made to maintain the integrity of each story, some content was truncated. If you are curious, or would like to delve deeper, each full episode is available on the Rebirth podcast.

As I wrote and rewrote these stories, there was an apparent synchronicity in the timing. It was as if each story held out its medicine to me when I needed it. I pray the same resonance finds you. Some stories may serve you more than others. Some may wait for you to share with a friend. Each story stands with honest wisdom, practical optimism, and radical assurance that where you are is purposeful and where you are going is possible, both with unseen and ever-present help awaiting to assist you.

Life is not a narrow line. Each day weaves forward and backward, just like this book, carrying the storyline along, weaving into the cosmos. My intention is that you will leave each chapter with a new gem in your pocket that may serve you on your own rebirth, whether you are contemplating a decision, sitting with a quest for understanding, or simply wanting to nourish yourself with the vitality of the human spirit. I welcome you to this new dawn, and I am glad you are here.

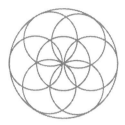

Expect Resistance and Watch for Serendipity

When the idea of the Rebirth podcast was germinating, I asked myself: Why? Who would listen? What would I have to talk about? And honestly, what was the point? Would it be worth it, and how would I know?

These are all valid questions as long as they do not silence the spark asking to be tended. Before becoming a mother, I said yes to a lot of things because I had the time and the personality for going everywhere. I was also in the season of life for the focus to be outward, to accrue experiences, and do, do, do. That doesn't condone saying yes to things I *know I don't want*. It means saying yes to learning what my relationship with life is. Asking why something is worth the precious and limited resource of our presence is a helpful and kind practice. It's an easy and effective way to take a moment and *be in the moment*—to learn and to trust that your yes is good and true, no matter how your landscape has changed, or how desperately you are waiting for change.

My present moment had changed. I went from being a traveling teacher to a very grounded mama, and I was learning life in a whole new way. And yet, that is not exactly true. You are who you are in every turn of a growth cycle—in every rebirth—but sometimes you can forget or lose yourself; it can take a moment to remember, to expand, to be with—or to learn the truth of—how amazing you are.

Where are you in your phase of living and growth, and how do you know when that phase has changed? Because it will. I wish we told more kids that things change—and to expect it. No matter your age, a better focus is knowing what is right for you in the present moment. Knowing what it feels like when a change is needed. Sometimes the best teachers are the things that don't work out. They are hard and necessary thresholds. They help us know what *is* in alignment.

I had this contemplation tucked into my brain for a bit while pondering whether I should take my friend Joe's (who you will meet later in the book) suggestion to make a podcast. A serendipitous answer arrived unexpectedly in the frozen food section of Whole Foods.

My sister has a Mary Poppins quality to her, as she beautifully whisks her kids through this adventure of life. She and her pack had recently arrived in Philadelphia for a visit while I was very much a new mother of one child. I was honestly intimidated to be navigating the crowd and the universe of children we had in our cart at the gargantuan Whole Foods on Pennsylvania Avenue in downtown Philly. There were so many people, and choices, and little beings to attend to... and I was not yet sturdy on my mothering legs.

At the end of one aisle was a categorically delightful human who had miniature popsicles in his hand, which he was passing out while explaining their sugar index (of basically no harm). So, we stopped and let the kids get one. We walked around the whole store, and the popsicles didn't drip at all. They were miniature in size yet deeply satisfying, so they didn't interfere with our shopping, and there were no deleterious effects of excessive sugar. I was astounded.

Just like that, the invitation came: This was what I wanted more of in the world. Humans doing and sharing things that would bring more good. Here was a product that *served* its customer instead of the customer having to rebound after consuming the product! I ran to the freezer section, grabbed two boxes, and had this thought: I'll reach out to Mompops. If they do an interview, I'll launch Rebirth.

Simple as that, I had a mission. I knew I wanted to share stories that were empowering and valuable to our everyday life—like this popsicle. To prove, to myself and my community, that we can live life another way. I kid you not—this was my gauntlet moment. I sent Mompops an enthusiastic DM on Instagram, and they accepted. Confirmation had arrived in my universe.

Rebirth was born.

Meet Stephanie Cohen

Stephanie Cohen is one of the three partners in Mompops. Before she became Chief Poperating Officer/co-owner of Mompops, she was Chief Operating Officer at Kremer Eye Center, a premier institution in Philadelphia, PA. Her background focus had been in healthcare operations, primarily in ophthalmology. This unique combination of knowledge bloomed when Stephanie worked in operations at Kremer. Her work ethic, supportive management style, and strategic, organizational visioning brought her much success and in turn demanded much of her—which she loved, until it was time for change.

Muscling ahead is neither right nor wrong; it's about knowing what is right for you in the moment, and these decisions are often not easy to see or to make. Stephanie talks fondly about her time and her mentor at Kremer. She left her job because it was time to move on, knowing she was no longer able to offer her job or her family her best self anymore:

> "I was so focused on my career and advancing it that I looked at my seven-year-old son and thought, *I don't know anything about you.* There were some changes in the organization occurring, and around that time, both my husband and my father were diagnosed with cancer within six months. Thankfully, they are both fine... but I told my boss, *I think I have reached my shelf life here, which isn't good for me and frankly not good for the organization.* It was time to start the next chapter of my life. What was it going to be?" Stephanie asked herself. "I had no idea."

She became involved in a local business cooperative located in a food incubator collaborative called Artisan Exchange in West Chester, PA. In short, they help businesses start with very low risk in the form of shared spaces so that the initial start-up for a business becomes manageable and oriented to be successful. Although it didn't work out for Stephanie in the long term, her time there most definitely served its purpose. Her physical placement in the building afforded her the opportunity to meet the founders of the company she would eventually become a partner in: Mompops.

Now, before we continue the journey forward with Stephanie, let me catch you up on Mompops, which is a vegan, allergen-friendly popsicle company. They are now located outside of Philadelphia in Kennett Square, PA, and beloved by the moms of the community. I learned this in real time. Whenever I mentioned I was chatting with the company, people's eyes lit up. *We love Mompops!* I heard again and again.

Although I do stand 100% behind this product, there is another reason I want to share the story of this company with you. Mompops' birth story is a testament to finding the thread of creation when life is handing you a new direction and demanding you follow it. Let's go into the story of Mompops' founders Issa Ostrander and his mom Sandy Ostrander, as shared with me by Stephanie. Let's begin at the relative beginning.

> "Issa graduated from high school, and both of his parents were entrepreneurs for most of their career. They decided to open a business together. They did some research and found Mom's Bake at Home pizza franchise," Stephanie explains, "and it was doing really well when they purchased it. However, shortly thereafter, the franchise sold to another group. They changed the recipe and started adding preservatives and lost a lot of customers."

Sidenote: I not only remember, but was personally disappointed and stopped going to Mom's Bake at Home because of this. But on with Stephanie's story:

"Additionally, the bake at home business was great in the wintertime, but in the summertime, no one wanted to turn on their ovens. So they had already lost 40% of the business when the weather got hot; add onto that the recipe changing—it was a recipe for disaster. So Issa and Sandy were looking for ways to pay the bills and offset the loss of income in the summer," Stephanie explains.

Sandy, at the time of the interview, was 73; Stephanie attests to her still having the deep, creative energy of a 25 year old. Let's take you back to Mompops' inspired evolution point:

"Sandy was at a fair. She was thirsty and got a popsicle. Afterwards, she said she was 'thirstier than when I ate it. It was infused with sugar, there is nothing refreshing about this,'" Stephanie recounts.

"An idea was born: popsicles as a summer treat to offset the winter loss. Sandy started tinkering in the kitchen. Her son, Issa, thought his mom's efforts were preposterous and was uninterested in her idea," Stephanie says.

Sandy made a few hundred popsicles, took them to the farmer's markets, and sold out. She did this a few weeks in a row, and her son began to change his mind about his mother's crazy idea.

That winter, Isssa dug in and watched every YouTube video he could and learned everything he could about popsicles, production, and equipment. He started testing the concept. Stephanie states that one year, Issa did 20 farmer's markets *a week*.

Stick with me, because this is the part of the story that I truly love and feel was medicine for my stubborn self that may help you, too. Issa started out with large popsicles, which as Stephanie mentions,

"is fine for the summer months. The first grocery store that he got placed in was Mom's Organic in Bryn Mawr, PA, and for demo'ing purposes in-store, he had a smaller, one-ounce pop."

People would say, "I love this, where can I get it?"

He'd show them the big popsicle box, and they would say, "Not in that size. I want this size."

He answered, "This is my sample size."

To which the potential customers responded, "When you start selling this size, I will buy it."

This is the moment Stephanie recounted that is profound to me. Can you remember a time when you were charging ahead, doing all that needed to be done, when a burst of wild inspiration comes in that you logically think is crazy? Yet crazy can lead to the most glorious, unexpected breakthroughs. It's that cross-section of hard work and grace. It's the moment that is larger than its parts, if you listen. It's what alignment looks like.

Stephanie affirms that their company is constantly evolving and fine-tuning to learn what works best: "If you aren't willing to do that, you aren't going to grow. You won't be successful."

So Issa began the migration to the mini-pop and landed in his first Whole Foods through Artisan Exchange in early 2015. Stephanie began working with him in late summer of 2015 with "no intentions of joining the company."

Ah, the magic of resistance when it meets serendipity is one of my favorite flavor combinations.

Stephanie was planning on heading back into healthcare with a new purview and a role that would allow her to spend more time with her family to help maintain that work-life balance that she had decided to reclaim for herself. Meanwhile, Issa was looking for a partner.

Stephanie was clear she wasn't going to move forward in that direction with Mompops, *but* Issa had made it on Shark Tank (per Stephanie's inspiration— remember, she is in Artisan Exchange, the same physical location as Issa). He needed help understanding his offered thousand-page contract, and

Stephanie agreed to help him sift through it. The biggest red flag she saw was that whether he "got a deal or didn't, Shark Tank would take a percentage of his gross revenue, so if you are okay with that, move forward. But what are you *really* looking for?" Stephanie asked Issa.

Issa answered that what he really wanted was someone to "roll up their sleeves and be in it every day with me."

Stephanie explained that this was not what was in front of him with Shark Tank. She told him she had a few weeks before she made her transition to something more full-time, so "why didn't she work with him for a little bit?"

Life. Interesting how it intercedes

For the moment, Stephanie started working with Issa, going to a few events, where

> "[she] saw the reaction people had to this product and how different it was from everything else out there on the market because it was something locally made, but it was free of so much junk," Stephanie says.

Issa's mom, a retired music teacher,

> "saw the increase in diabetes diagnosis and obesity, and she saw the segregation that came with the kids that couldn't have peanuts or tree nuts, or had dietary restrictions, so she wanted to create something that had great flavor, used real ingredients that could fill you up, but was free of the ingredients that created the segregation. So that is really where the premise came from," Stephanie shares.

I think you taste it. I think you can taste Sandra Ostrander's inclusive and loving intention in her popsicles. I think it was what got people's attention; it got *my* attention that harried morning in Whole Foods. It got Stephanie Cohen's attention, even when she wanted to resist it. With service as foundation, the ability to grow and thrive is endless—for everyone.

I didn't know all of this when I sent that Instagram message asking Mompops to be on my almost-birthed podcast. And yet this one popsicle carried the same energy of my intention, a cross-section of purpose. When you read through these stories of Rebirth, I hope you allow yourself and your ideas to be included. I hope you let your resistance squawk and choose to turn up your faith as you notice yourself in those that rise up to greatness, hop on a plane to destiny, walk away from one great thing because they know they are called to another, or wait for a decade for their mission to reveal itself. It is my prayer that you let the idea that there is another way that is collaborative and fun, profitable and powerful be available to you. Whether your goals are professional or personal, finding true alignment matters. You deserve it, and you are ready to birth it now.

Choose to turn up your faith.

"You can always make it work, if you want it bad enough," is the motto that Stephanie lives and works by. She doesn't consider herself an entrepreneur. She does consider Issa one. She considers herself "a hard worker, task-oriented, operations person through and through," she laughs.

> "I've gone through so much corporate training, Nordstrom and The Don DiJulius Group, but it's all about your customer. This is who you do it for, so you should provide exceptional service," she clearly emphasizes, and she means it. "I wanted to bring that to the organization. Issa loves making pops. It is his thing. I bring more of the business background, the discipline. We both strategize. He oversees the back end. Every pop that goes out of there, he sees or touches. I am more finance, marketing, and sales growth. It is really a great partnership. His mom still comes in almost every single day and makes pops with him."

So what made Stephanie commit to Mompops?

"Oh," Stephanie explains, "it was definitely gradual." Partly the uniqueness of the product and her consciousness of mindful eating over the last 20 years in her own life, and partially inspired by the diabetes that runs through her family. The fulcrum moment was in December of 2015, when she got the call that her three-year-old nephew was diagnosed with Type 1 Diabetes.

"To manage Type 1," Stephanie explains, "it is a maintenance of diet. Eating three times a day, and if you eat between meals, they want you to keep it to under five grams of carbs, which is basically carrots and cucumbers—but these pops met that criteria. As I got more and more involved, I realized that these pops, something so simple, were making an impact on my brother and sister-in-law. My sister-in-law told me, 'I know it's silly, but he loves these pops, and it is just one less thing to think about.' And that sealed it for me. And we do a lot with JDRF because of that. I can't help my nephew. I can't make him better. This is how I can have an impact.

"One day in February, we got an email, which we thought was spam," Stephanie says in an aside, "saying they needed 300,000 pops in eight weeks. I thought, I'll return the email and see what kind of hoax this is. Well, it turns out it wasn't. It was a large, national day camp that waited until the last minute to place their order. Most day camps need an allergen-friendly pop. He was having a tough time finding it, and a company in California said they couldn't scale to that order, but she knew a company that could and gave him our name. Issa said, 'That's more than I made in the last five years.' And I was like, 'Yeah, well we are going to do it.'

"And we did it," Stephanie laughs. "We had just moved into a new facility. It was insane. We were working 24/7. I still do healthcare consulting, so there were times we would work until

2 am. I'd get home around 2:45 am, sleep for two hours, go work ten hours of consulting, go back to the shop, and Issa is still working. It was the craziest eight to ten weeks we ever had, but we did it. I still remember our pallets—16,144 pops per pallet out to California, with some on the East Coast. We had never shipped that far, but we did it. We went from there and never looked back." She laughs again. "I had been dragging my heels on the partnership papers for a while. I think one day during that, I finally signed the papers and left it on the back table for him. He walked in and said, 'Alright?' I said, 'Yep, alright.' And we have been hustling ever since."

I had to ask, why does Stephanie still stay and hustle?

She laughs. "Every day I probably would give you another answer. But you know what? I believe in the product. And we have invested so much," is her answer.

"I've spent most of my career in healthcare," she continues. "If I didn't think I was helping anyone with this product, I wouldn't be here. Listen, once you learn operations, you can do operations anywhere. While it's not restoring vision or trying to ensure people's vision doesn't get worse, it is delivering to people that provides a benefit to them. That has always been very important to me, ensuring that whatever I did I had an impact in people's lives in some way, shape, or form.

"You know," she continues, "I also love rules and processes, and there [are] a lot of regulations in food production as well, obviously. We have a certified facility. It was not mandated when we did it, but we wanted to ensure that customers who purchased our product knew exactly what they were getting. Our demographic is kids," her voice softens, "so it's a high-risk population, and it has morphed into adults who are looking for a better option.

"You asked why I stayed," she says, "starting your own business is crazy highs and crazy lows. We spent three to four years building a really strong foundation and learning how to be in partnership together. Sometimes we have grown in light-years, and sometimes we wonder why we aren't where we thought we would be. But this year, this is the year where all the hard work is all coming together."

"And what about that work-life balance? We see so many articles about how to achieve it, what would you honestly say?" I ask.

"I haven't found it," she replies honestly. "It's not easy, and I have a great support system. I work all the time, and in the day to day, I am not great, but I keep my commitments to my son. And when he comes home from school, I close the computer. On the stuff that is really important to him, I am present. I am not answering my emails while I am talking to him. You have to pick and choose what is important to you. He and I go away once a year, since he's been five; we go and spend a week with my mom and dad. If he and his friends want to go somewhere, I drive him. You find ways that they see you are present. That you are part of their life."

As we talk on about the ever-changing goal of work-life balance, Stephanie shares,

"I've even made some changes in my life for me. I used to get up and go, go, go, but now I get up, make myself a cup of green tea and some yogurt with fresh berries, and I sit at my counter and read ten pages of this book I am reading (which incidentally was *Think and Grow Rich*). When I was a kid, I would come down in the morning, and I would see a cup of tea and an empty yogurt container. I told my mother, 'I'm turning into you!' Since I have done this, I feel better during the day. I am sleeping better. I feel like I am balancing things better because I am taking ten or fifteen minutes in the morning to just ease into my day versus run, run, run."

So we cannot have it all—but we can attend to our priorities.

As I thanked Stephanie for giving us a peek into a company that lives its values and its mission, she shared,

> "One more thing actually just popped up. It helped me more in the beginning, and I do go back to it. My grandfather, who my son is named after, Emmanuel Diamond, he was just an incredible person. We idolized him. Family was everything to him." You can hear the smile growing in her voice as she continues, "He was a hard-working dentist in a small town in central Pennsylvania. He worked all the time. He was my mother's father. When I struggled over the years with 'I'm not around' or 'I'm not this,' my mother said to me: 'Steph, you know my father meant everything to me. He wasn't around a lot. He worked a lot. But when he was there, he was there. It is not about the quantity of time you are with your loved one, it is the quality. When you are there, be there.' That helped me a lot."

Emmanuel Diamond left a beloved legacy that Stephanie carries as a reminder: that the presence she can give her family is all that she really needs to give. That same presence and passion was found in Sandy Ostrander teaching her son and teaching her school students. Who could have predicted that these fated cross-sections of commitment and destiny would be the backstory of a popsicle? It is the greatest metaphor for staying true to your dreams while being open to the miraculously unexpected that arrives on the wings of serendipity.

When a new vision comes, when a new challenge arises, if we stand on the foundation of serving others and being present, possibilities are endless. The invitation and the arrival make much more sense. Whether we are looking to those that inspired us or those that we aim to inspire, both the past and the future hold the foundational keys for what is to come.

Nowhere To Go But Up

When it all falls apart, there is no plan that works, no roadmap—no road. In fact, life takes on a malleable almost vertiginous property to it. I have had everything fall apart a few times myself to varying degrees. It announces itself through prickly tension in my temple and the heat in my forehead when I can feel that in the next moment, life will change irrevocably.

When the falling apart happens, it matters what is falling. It is easy to wax philosophical in the safety of my slippers, sipping nettle tea by candlelight (I light a candle when I write). It is much more difficult standing in the rubble of life's debris. The experiences of loves lost are relatable places to excavate these growth points together. There were two men I thought I was going to marry, and I married neither. One was in my twenties and another was in my thirties, and now I can look back and see that they were unable to cross the next threshold life was offering me, and I was subconsciously ready to move on. In both instances, although very different, I was catapulted deeper into the mysteries of life and further away from the predictability that I both craved and resisted.

The first break up was right before my Saturn return (Google it), just after I had secured my first teaching job and yoga teaching gig. I was stepping into an unknown archetype in my life, and instead of picking out homes and engagement rings, my solitude would begin seven years of worldly travel and end with me leaving traditional teaching and moving out to a little island in the Pacific. The second break up was more disorienting internally. It made me question myself, my worth, and my approach to relationships. It would take a much longer time to recover because it was less about the relationship and more about a need for internal growth throughout all corridors of my life and perception.

When our inner stability is shaken, the entanglement is further reaching and more confusing to understand and ultimately unwind. This chapter *is* about relationships: to yourself, for what you claim is your deep worth and lovability, and it is never, ever too late for that. Through the reshuffling of choice, we can pick a different path. We are on trajectories, and when we are catapulted off of them, honestly, there is no going back. You are different. The edifice has cracked, and if you learned your lesson, you are the better for it. If not, another learning opportunity will find its way to you.

When the drop comes, when we are the ones at the bottom, we can look up and wonder why. We can pretend it's not as bad as it is. We can blame. We can rant that we are not where we are supposed to be and no one has it harder than us—or we can get up. It's mostly a mash-up of it all. The rise eventually comes. Letting it come can often look like the deepest, ugliest surrender you can muster. Birth is not easy. It is messy and hard. It doesn't have to be, but it often is. They say the more you surrender to the pressure, the easier the ride. I say there are some people who live stories that give you the courage to rise up into your own.

Meet Christina Super Friedland

Christina Super Friedland is a woman of strength; it is in her eyes. I love her grit and grace, yet what I admire the most is the choice she makes to love— herself, others, and life itself—with wild faith. You can feel it in her presence. At the time of the podcast recording, she was pregnant with her third child and living a pinnacle moment of personal reclamation.

Christina has been in skincare for 24 years, and we were sitting in the newly opened, gorgeously elegant, booked-out location of her own skincare office. She talks about skincare being more than skincare. It is her way to share a loving craft, a guided touch that serves her customers holistically. In her office space, Christina has a wall of handcrafted paper flowers. A cascade of muted rose and quiet purples, spilling down the wall of the foyer, setting a subtle tone for beauty, as does Christina with her smart, redheaded bob haircut and her Chanel loafers ending an all-black outfit. Her understanding of luxury is obvious and welcoming.

Before opening this space, Christina had spent 21 years at the same establishment. When I ask her initially why she left, she solidly responds, "It was no longer portraying who I was."

A year before leaving, she noticed that although she loved her work, the environment was eroding her love for her work. It wasn't enough to do what she loved if it was in a place that did not value her.

"What was one of the indications that you were no longer in the right place?" I ask.

> "My favorite thing to do is one-on-one with the client... It's my comfort. It's an energy. It's a feeling. It's a vibe," Christina effuses. "And I wasn't feeling that anymore. About a year before I left, I started to pay attention to people who had passions. I knew I loved what I did. I mean, I *loved* it. But I was not loving my space anymore. I wanted to take it to the next level and have it be more one-on-one. And I felt like the industry was starting to steer away from that," she says. "I didn't want to do bigger and better."

"Why do you think that is?" I ask.

"Bigger-better," she repeats as her answer, with a knowing shrug of her shoulders.

"Oh, like everything else, and here," I motion to her office, "you have brought us to the intimate."

"Yes, this is who I am," she says, and her spine straightens as she melds a bit with the space.

There are clean lines and bold welcomes that adorn her office in an understated way. We sit in two high-backed grey chairs for the conversation, and behind Christina is a closed door where she sees her clients. "I had gained enough knowledge, learned enough on my own that I wanted to be able to share what *I* had and what *I* learned with other people."

"Yes," I empathize. "A lot of times we are told bigger-better is how it has to happen, but nature works in cycles. Something grows, it blossoms, and then it goes back down to begin the cycle again. It doesn't mean our career has to end; it means we move in cycles. We can't always have bigger-better growth. We have spirals," I go off on a bit of a tangent. "I think when we don't evaluate our life, we may be constantly guided to bigger-better, and not realize that we might have gone off track. So it sounds to me like you were listening to your internal compass."

"Yes," she says, smiling.

"Now there is more going on here than you just leaving." I lean in and make eye contact with her. "Let's talk about your journey. You know what it is like to have bigger-better, then have that disappear and have to rebuild. Would you share a bit about that with us?"

> "I was married very young, 21," she begins, "and very naïve, and went into a world that looked to me bigger-better, and I think it did to other people, too. I learned," she pauses carefully, "to go with that world. But there was always something in me that was missing. It was like this little voice. It was definitely not the healthiest environment. I had two children, and they were most important to me."

I nod my head, acknowledging her mothering came first.

> "As their mom and a woman, I worked part time. I took care of my children, and I didn't have much control over anything else in

my life. That's pretty much it. I did as I was directed to do," she punctuates with simplicity.

I let her chosen details fill the space and nod my head again for her to continue.

"I got to a point at about 34—I knew I was dying inside. Like I knew there wasn't going to be much left of me as a person if I stayed in an unhealthy environment, and I wanted my children to see better and to know we create our own lives. I know we hear that so much, but—I lived it. I get it," she explains. "I guess from the outside, it all looked great. I had nice things. A nice house. A nice car. But inside, I always said there was this void. I paid attention to it. At one point, I realized it's time to go—and it was not easy."

"I can't imagine it would be easy," I say.

"It wasn't. And it was not *made* easy for me," she clarifies succinctly, the statement carrying its own weight. "I lost everything."

"Sometimes it can be harder, when you have a lot to leave," I offer.

She nods in confirmation, legs crossed.

"Because everyone around you thinks you are crazy," I add with my hands circling in the air. "It looks like you have everything you need! Why leave?"

"100%," Christina agrees. She adds, "even in your own brain. Especially if you're told things like: *This is it. No one else is gonna want you. You don't make enough money.* You know, things that are hard. You are so scared of the unknown," Christina continues, "then you get to a point—at least for me, I did—that the unknown becomes less scary than the familiar."

"How did that feel?" I ask. "I'm hearing that you maintained an internal connection with yourself. Did the voice you mention get louder or quieter...?"

"It literally screamed," she exclaims, and we both laugh in relief and recognition. Christina expands, "And at that time, you want the voice to shut up. You *want* to shut it up; for years, I wanted it to shut up. You don't know what's on the other side. You don't know how you are going to do it. You don't know where you are going to go. But when you get to that point—there's a point," she leans in, "and for everybody it's different, but for me, that point was: *What am I doing? What am I living?* I am not being authentic to who I am. I am not living my best life. I am not being who I know I am inside."

"What did that look like?" I ask.

"For me, I had to leave with my children. A year of living with my parents—I would have to borrow a car each day from my dad, my mom, or my brother, to drop my kids at school. Meanwhile, I am still going to work" she continues, "and I am trying to figure out what's next. With children involved, I tried to keep it all together for them. I was a 35-year-old woman out in the world, and divorce is hard."

"No matter what," I say.

"No matter what," she agrees. "But when you have other external battles going on with it—it's harder," she intimates.

We talk about how the world can be unkind and fearful about divorce, but there can be unsuspecting grace, too—from people or moments you would have never imagined. I asked her, "What do you think your kids learned from this?"

Christina answers immediately: "Resilience. 100%, and I am proud of this. One thing I asked myself—and I still do this to this day—what is my intent? When I do something, I ask myself, *What is my intent?* And if I can honestly answer that my intent is good, then I am good with it. I'm okay sharing my story," she smiles at me, "or talking to people, because we are all in this together—we hope. It helps me make my decisions and to keep going, especially that one year of the divorce process."

"Tell me the story about the floor," I ask her abruptly.

"I was in my sister's bedroom because my daughter wanted my bedroom, and we couldn't fit the box spring up the steps, so it was just the mattress on the floor. One day, I was laying on the bed. I remember laying there and looking up at the ceiling and thought, *I am in so much pain.* Emotional pain. I remember thinking to myself, *I wonder if it would hurt more if I just rolled myself onto the floor, more than what I am feeling inside right now.* So I rolled myself onto the floor—fortunately it was just from the mattress onto the floor—and I laid there.

"But I remember my first thought was, *That hurt.* The second thought was, *I am as low as I am gonna go.* I just rolled myself onto the floor. I have no car, no house. I have two children I am trying to raise, I'm still working part-time trying to get more work, and I don't know where tomorrow is. I don't know where we are going to live in a year. I have no idea what's going to happen.

"And then there was this moment," she says, looking at me. "They say you get those moments. I got this rush of peace. At the moment, I realized the void I had all those years was gone. I didn't feel it anymore. After that, I realized I didn't lose every-thing. I gained everything because I was officially me. No more hiding, no more this or that. It didn't matter anymore. Nothing mattered. I had nowhere to go but up because I was on the floor. Literally."

I love this story so much. When we delude ourselves about how bad, or how good, something is, we cannot change it. There is a tradeoff, a price for reclamation, and it takes courage to pay it.

"So the void is gone," I say. "Talk to us about the slow steps to the turnaround, because the feeling is everything."

> "That feeling was amazing. There wasn't an endless bank account," she says, grounding us into reality. "I was fortunate that I had my parents to live with. At some point, you realize you gotta get up. You can sit on that floor for a moment, but you gotta get up. It's not easy. And just when I think I cannot do it anymore, that little flicker would come back, and I would keep going. Slowly but surely, I kept going.

> "I believe in something bigger than me, and that helped me," she says. "And gratitude. I really started to pay attention to things to be grateful for. Gratitude made all the difference. I know it is cliché, but it did. Like, the people that I thought over the years that would be with me that didn't come through—that didn't matter. What did matter was the people that did. Like, people you didn't even know that were paying attention would call me up and say: *Hey, you okay?* You have no idea the power of that and what that can do for someone's day."

I appreciate her piercing honesty. "Thank you," I say. "That is one of my core beliefs. That your story can help someone else."

Christina jumps right in:

> "That is huge. As crazy as it sounds, I remember thinking in those moments to myself that someday this will help someone else. This," she motions to the podcast, "is all part of that—that we are all here to help the next, so maybe this is my turn," she says, smiling.

I melt a bit, appreciating the confluence of two intentions finding each other—a moment where the flicker of connection and inspiration brightens.

Around a year and a half after moving in with her parents, Christina moved her family into a new home. She was confident they would be able to manage this new life, albeit a little tenuously, and in came a mascot to lead the way. A five-year-old dog needing an immediate home to escape being put down caught Christina's attention on social media. She asked for a five-day deferral as she was in the middle of moving, and the dog foster agreed. Christina shares that the first night in the new home with no furniture, she and the dog slept on two yoga mats. Two rebounding souls ready for a new home and a new life.

> "I was still working in skincare, and I was starting to really drop into the idea of being comfortable in my own skin. I wasn't looking for a new partner. When my kids were out, I had my dog," she says, shrugging her shoulders happily.

As they settled into the new home, Christina began to settle into herself. She was also getting acclimated to the idea that maybe she didn't need much more. She could date when her kids weren't around, but maybe it was okay to leave that part of life alone—shortly after this acceptance, she met her fiancé Brad.

> "Brad was like the dog," she says affectionately of them both. "Years before, somebody told me I was going to meet someone that was nothing like I had known before. That always stuck in my head—and there he was. It was easy and effortless. Before, in the dating world, I was trying to be eight different women because I didn't know who I was."

"Why do we women do that?" I let my head tilt as the question slips out.

> "I don't know. I was out there meeting people, trying to fit into who this person wants me to be, and I thought, *Wait a minute. Why would I go back to doing that again?* And I admit my behavior was crazy because I didn't know what else to do. When I met Brad," her tone softened, "it was just easy. I didn't have a reason to stop dating him. Then slowly but surely, over a few months, I'm like..." and her voice trails off.

I would venture to say that her face had a reminiscent whisper of her perplexity about how good and easy life with Brad grew to be.

Christina comes back to the moment and shares, "Just the little things. His kindness. He's good. I couldn't even believe this existed as we went on. And then he met my dog, and the dog loved him. The dog *didn't* love everybody."

As her mothering self, she made a careful choice to get to know him before he was introduced to her kids. In talking with Christina about her newly rebirthed self in relationship, she says:

> "When it is a true and fulfilling relationship, you are just you. He helps me be me. I learned how important that was in a relationship. He had been divorced for several years, too. Both of us were at a point where we were okay with who we were, so there was no more pretend. We just were."

"How did Brad play a role in you rebirthing your business?" I ask.

"He believed in me. He believed in me more than I believed in myself. I didn't plan on leaving."

"Your job?" I ask. "Even though you knew it wasn't right?"

I have this problem, shall we say, that I cannot always hold my equanimity in an interview. If something shocks me, I say it. If something reminds me of a tangent, I often run down it before reeling myself in, so although I knew there were entanglements with Christina's work, I had not put all the pieces together that her marriage and her work had entwinements. When I heard the story of her picking herself and her life up off of the floor, I was a bit shocked that it took her that much longer to leave her job, but that was because I was listening to her story and not living it. I can now see that there are so many perplexing polarities in life. We can be clear and confused. We can need time and patience for unwinding and truly setting ourselves free.

"Yeah, I paid attention," she remarks. "Again, it was a stirring, but just like my marriage, I didn't know where to go."

And there you have it. The place where we think there may only be one pattern, we realize another may have threaded through. Luckily, when you pull a thread, the unraveling reveals its origin.

"But what was the step that got you to leave?" I ask.

"Things were changing."

"Okay," I press, "from a business side, what was one of your first steps? Was it walking around a neighborhood look[ing] for a location, was it—"

"A panic attack," she drops like a hot, flat truth.

I laugh at the force of the statement, but then the look in her eye lands, and I draw back into the reality of what she said.

"No really, on my way to work. A bad one," Christina says.

"I had no idea," I said.

"Yeah, I had to call 911 on myself. I thought I was having a heart attack."

I am pitch-still, silent.

> "Yeah, because of some things—" she lets a boundaried silence land, and I don't press. She then continues, as open and honest as she had been when she talked about rolling onto the floor or finding a rescue dog to love. "I was driving, and I never had this happen. I pulled over and called 911, and an ambulance came and got me."

"I had no idea," I offered again.

"Yeah, I go big," she says in stride. "I hold on until the very last second, until someone kicks me and says, 'You got to go.'"

"So the ambulance came—"

> "Yeah, and took me to the hospital. Brad came. The results of my test came back, and the doctor told me I had a severe panic attack.

They were gonna see what was causing these things. So yeah, we went home, and I remember before the panic attack, when I was driving to work—I know this sounds funny—I literally felt like someone was pushing me back. Like, I can't get there. I'm not supposed to get there," she explains.

"Brad and I had a talk, and he said, 'This is killing you. You are not going to be good to anyone if you get sick because of all the things," she motions with her hand, "that can go on inside someone when they are in an unhealthy environment. This isn't good for you anymore.'

"Again, I thought, *What do I do?* I have two children. They are in private school. These are things I had worked for, you know?" Christina says.

I nod.

"Brad said, 'You have to quit.' But I thought, *I don't quit. I don't have a Plan B. I mean, I have never quit a job. How do you do this?*"

Change can take time to ripple through the spiral of your being. It ends up not as obvious as we think, and yet it is exactly that simple. I find that when you honor a pause, it often tells you everything you truly need to know.

"So I did." She pauses. "I resigned."

With a new smile on her face, Christina shares, "I woke up the next morning, I sat in my egg chair with my journal, and I looked around and thought: *Oh my God, what am I going to do with the rest of my life?* But the only thing I did know was what I learned from before. That this was a blessing. These moments of, *I don't know what in God's green Earth I am going to do next.* But it comes. Somehow, it comes. Somehow, someway, it comes. It does.

"You just gotta put the effort in." Her voice drops into her signature grit and determination. "I started reaching out to people. I put a resume together, and, well, I knew I wanted to be in the city—New York or Philly or both. I am used to working in a dark room all day, so to put myself out there was, 'Waaaah!'" she laughs.

"Oh," I understood, "that's a threshold."

Although pounding the pavement for a new job worked in that she received numerous offers, they weren't much better than what she already had. Missing her work, Christina decided to rent a little space of her own in downtown Philadelphia to do facials. None of her clients of 21 years knew where to find her, so she had to start from scratch. That point perplexed me, so I clarified, "Because you were working for a company, and they retained client records?"

"Yes, that and my old company told my clients that I had retired."

I blinked. It was like every aspect of her life had been wiped away. She met a wonderful woman that rented Christina space hourly in a city office. She would hang her sign out on the door for the hours that she was there, then tuck her sign into her bag on her way home until the next day. Eventually, her clientele's demand outgrew her hourly availability, and she grew into a perfect place at 16th and Walnut that was peaceful, precious, and hers—it's where we are sitting now.

When stories of great change happen, they rarely happen linearly.

When stories of great change happen, they rarely happen linearly. There is often a sashaying back and forth, a mindful or subconscious unearthing of patterns and perspectives that need to be massaged to make way for what is finding its way to you. Hitting the floor is allowing the depth to rise to its reciprocal growth. It is an equation I have heard repeated in the stories of those that embrace what life is waiting to offer.

Months after this interview, I saw a picture of Christina and Brad's wedding on Zoom during the pandemic, surrounded by their children. All of them shined, the newlyweds and the children alike, in love with each other and with life. The cycles of rebirth are always available to us. Like Christina says, "You just gotta put in the work, and somehow, someway, it comes."

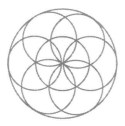

This Life Is for You

When I was little, I was fascinated with the idea that I needed someone else to tell me what was wrong with my body. I remember learning about my organs in anatomy and physiology, looking at my body, and wondering why I couldn't talk to them. What did the doctor know that I didn't, and why would my body talk to my doctor and not me? It's intriguing what the innocent mind can question, and how we let children climb and tumble through ideas.

I was never interested in being a doctor though. I was always interested in stories. For my senior project, I wrote my research paper on documented medical miracles. I found this paper in a cardboard box in my thirties, and I was shocked at myself. It was like my younger self was winking at me, waiting to be remembered. What did I know then that I had forgotten since?

First, nothing is lost. Sometimes we forget so that we can truly learn. As we will discuss more in our chat with Joe Longo, all we need to do is remember, and it is that remembering and forgetting and remembering again that seems to be an essential piece of our very human learning. But what about the unplannable turns that life has for all of us? Here, we are going to talk about Lisa O'Rear's story; her brilliant radiance of being is a call for us all to remember—or more accurately, listen—to our bodies, no matter what the world outside is telling us.

The great thing about learning, the real art of practicing a new skill, is doing it *before* it is needed. Let Lisa take you on a journey that reminds all of us to listen to ourselves, to remember that we have an innate knowing of who and what we are—and from there, seek out the support we need. And at a very real and necessary level, tune in to your body. Practice your alignment. When you have an inner knowing, even when everyone around you says you are wrong, practice knowing what your clarity sounds like. One more thing that ends up being *the thing*: life happens. No matter our planning or knowing, some journeys present regardless; may we walk them with as much resilience and beauty as Lisa does.

Meet Lisa O'Rear

Sometime or other, we find ourselves at a crossroads, a moment in our path that is unpredictable and unknowable. As Lisa O'Rear says: "It's not if, it's when." Lisa, now and again a Floridian, teaches alignment-based yoga. When our paths crossed, she was teaching in Philadelphia, PA and was looking to share and write her story. She mentioned off-handedly that she cannot do a bunch of fancy yoga stuff, and she shared with me, as she will with you, the breadth of her journey to yoga. Lisa brings a clear elegance to all that she does. She brightens a room when she talks, and she holds a strict line on getting things done. You can trace it in her voice and admire it in her perspective on life. It is a great combination for a yoga teacher: expansive and grounded.

As we chatted, we talked about why and how it is yogic to do yoga for one's actual body type and phase of life:

> "I'm an alignment-based teacher because of my backstory. But basically it's [that] where you put your hands and your feet matters. How you stack your joints matters. Don't get me wrong, I love to flow and move; however, I'm also 43 years old, and my body no longer moves the way it did when it was 23. So the idea

of a pulled hamstring in your twenties—you probably heal a little bit faster than you do when you are in your forties. It is really important to find that balance between engagement, like strength and flexibility."

Lisa delineates. "At the end of the day, we all age. If we don't age, the alternative is that we are not here anymore. So how do we keep up with our ever-changing bodies?"

"Oh, I hear that. It's just the truth," I agree.

"I don't feel good every morning, but I get the opportunity to give it another go. When I step on my mat, the idea is, *I get to do this*. It's gonna look different everyday and feel different everyday. Different parts of me are gonna be tighter than yesterday, or they will be tomorrow. The idea is, *I am so grateful I still get to do it*."

You can feel it in her voice—the commitment to meeting life on the mat. It isn't until later that I connect that she is choosing not to name her chronic pain and that her appreciation for still moving her body is a visceral, day-to-day experience.

"So let's talk about that," I suggest, opening the door to her story.

"Yes, let's do it," she says open-heartedly. "In 2011, I had a stroke. I was 34 years old. As a result of it, I don't feel the left side of my body. Part of my stroke got into my brainstem, which obviously controls all automatic functions; it controls pain sensations, temperature sensations, swallowing, coughing, sneezing—it's all that automatic system. So the yoga I practiced before is not the yoga I practice now, simply because I cannot feel like I used to. And so I found this yoga. For the first time, I was like, *Wow, I can do this and move and not hurt myself.* I still want to practice. I want to teach. How do I do it on a very basic level and stay safe? Having a stroke at 34 can kinda blow your mind. It's so funny. I share it with people; I am very open about it. The more you know, the

more empowered you can be to be able to recognize symptoms…
but I never know how to open the subject."

We laugh a bit. Humans laugh at the sacred, and they laugh at the profane.
They laugh to diffuse a moment that they need to open to because it is still a
story of *her* life and *her* loss and *her* rising again. The tenacity with which Lisa
lives and shares her story and her unwavering commitment to being heard
knocks me over in awe. Because, as she reminds us, we get to do this thing
called life. We get to, again and again.

One of the first responses she received, when she said something was wrong,
was that she was ignored—by the medical professionals.

> "Yes. I went into the hospital for a standard procedure, in and
> out. A colonoscopy and an endoscopy. If at 34 you're wondering
> why I did that, I had some symptoms, and I had acid reflux for
> years, and the doctors were like, 'If we are going to do one, we
> should do both.' And I said, 'Okay, great.'
>
> "So I go in, and the first hint that I had—do you ever get the
> feeling? Where it is just like, something does not feel right, just
> in your gut? You can't explain it. I just chalked it up to, *Well,
> nobody likes to go under, so I'm just anxious about that.* I was
> supposed to be in and out. I didn't bring anything with me.
> In and out.
>
> "I ended up having a reaction to a medicine that they [gave] me
> prior to anesthesia, so I actually never had the procedure. But it
> caused my heart rate to shoot up, my blood pressure to shoot up.
> I had a tachycardia, [which abruptly stopped the procedure].
> After all of these symptoms, I remember telling multiple people
> as they took me back into recovery: 'Something doesn't feel
> right.' I'm having this horrible pain in my neck and in my arm,
> and it's traveling, and nobody listened to me. Multiple doctors. It
> was a long, seven-day journey…"

When they admitted Lisa post-operation, it was to the general floor, not neurology or cardiology. Lisa told the attending physician that she thought she was having a stroke, and he asked her to explain her physical symptoms, which were coincidentally in alignment with what she knew of strokes from her previous work as a medical paralegal. When she finished, Lisa recalls him laughing and dismissing her since she was only 34.

Perhaps you are, like I was, shocked that they didn't listen to her. I asked Lisa to clarify: Who was it that wasn't listening?

"It started with the doctor in the recovery room, and the anesthesiologist, who I refer to as a proud racehorse, who kept throwing his head up and saying, 'No, no, you're fine.' And they took me to the ER, and it was the ER doctor. She said to me: 'Oh no, you're just thin. You're just tired, exhausted, scared, and dehydrated.'" Lisa groans at the reasons and ridiculousness (my word) with which she was dismissed.

And this was the beginning of "seven days of saying something isn't right?" I ask.

> Lisa restates, "What I kept hearing was: 'You're a 34-year-old woman.' There was no reason that I should have had a stroke. I had low blood pressure. I have a strong heart. I was a runner, I tried my best to live a healthy lifestyle. I just kept hearing, 'You're 34.'
>
> "Okay. So that means there is no realm of possibility that I'm having a stroke?" she asks boldly for all of us. "In my former life I was a paralegal, and I did medical malpractice defense. I spent 18 years poring over medical records, and I kept feeling like they thought I was trying to tell them how to do their job. And that was not it!" she explains, and I hear her.

The question arises in my mind: How many times do we need to tell a story? As many times as it needs to be heard, I think. Lisa isn't alone. Although different, we can turn towards our own lives and see many places where we are told that we don't know what is best, even when we do. Hers is a story that invites us to reflect more deeply. It beckons to us: How do we align inner authority over our external authority? Where do we exert ourselves? Where do we trust and follow another's decisions over our existence? How do we know which of those moments we are in? How do we sit inside of ourselves, and what do we do when we are vulnerable and not heard? What does personal autonomy, personal sovereignty, look like in our day to day? How do you prepare for the unknowable? How do you advocate for yourself for seven days when no one is paying attention?

"Well, to be fair, it was three and a half days, and then they sent me home unable to really walk. I really couldn't see out of my right eye. I had a drooping right side of my face—but what's interesting is, I passed my neuro exam. Which I don't even understand how I did, but I did. So they sent me home.

"I just remember I couldn't walk when I left the hospital. They say when you have a stroke, you lose your balance. When I say you lose your balance—it is not like, *Oh, I'm, like, dizzy, I lost a step*. No, no, no. You cannot stand straight up. It's literally like something is dragging you down to the side. I remember I was just holding on to the wall as I was walking out because my husband, then fiancé, had to go get the car. I remember the nurse with me; she was the only person that was like, 'This is not right; I can't believe they are letting you go home.'

"So then I ended up going home because I was exhausted and I was sobbing. They kept telling me it was a migraine. Ended up the next day having *way* more symptoms, like projectile vomiting... It was ugly. I ended up going back to another ER in another hospital. Because all of our medical systems are linked in Philadelphia, they had a record that I was literally just discharged from another hospital. So they took me back immediately, and within hours, they had figured out that I had a stroke, but it was 72 hours from when it initially happened.

"I am so grateful to be alive. Because when—" She steps back in her words to graciously educate us. "So basically, I had all of the textbook symptoms. I kinda was at the end of my rope, and the next step would have been a coma because it was in my brainstem. It started in my cerebellum. The clot blocked the blood flow, not only to my cerebellum, but started to get into my brainstem, which is why I have what is—I'll do air quotes—wrong with me now. But nobody listened."

Sometimes stories are so big that when they are told and retold, we as listeners can be served by slowing down into the pauses of what is not said, what weight is not shared with us. Lisa has educated me, and I hope I have honored some of that in the fine line of learning and respecting what a stroke survivor, or thriver, goes through—yet not solely identifying them with that, or *as* that. No one wants to be labeled as "what is wrong with me" (as Lisa delineated in air quotes for our ease of inner knowing). Let us hold the reverence for the journey and the tenacity rather than slipping into the categorization of a human as one thing, one event.

"Literally nobody listened," Lisa reiterates. "And part of me has all of this regret that I should have listened more to myself and been louder, been more of an advocate for myself. But to be quite honest, I had never had to be an advocate for myself, and this was a hard lesson to learn. But I will never make that mistake again. I am grateful for the experience, even though it's been a very challenging nine years. I joke that it is the best and worst thing that has happened to me—learning to speak up."

"It probably forced something in you to grow," I offer, still opening to the scale of her story.

"I remember saying multiple times, 'Something is really not right.' And I just remember apologizing for it. What is that? Why do we do that? Why do we apologize?" Lisa asks us.

I pick up her line of questioning with my own reflections. "One of the reasons I wanted to share your story—not only of your own personal courage—but to shake that rug for all of us about medical advocacy. Whether it's your dentist, or my C-section, or being judged, everyone is human. I think there is something going on where it is really easy to not hear people or listen to their individual perspectives, and your story is such a glaring example of the dangers of not slowing down to listen."

> Lisa clarifies, "Every time I said something, I always prefaced it with that: 'Hey, I know I am not in charge here, I am just telling you that the symptoms that I am having are textbook stroke.' I'm not trying to be a smartass, but let's be fair. When you have a colonoscopy, you don't eat for the entire day before. You just drink liquids and that really gross stuff so they can clean out your system. So my point is... I was exhausted," she says. "I was trying so hard, even my husband was trying so hard to get them to pay attention, and I think it's almost..." and she takes a moment to come back to being kind even in telling her own story. "Listen, I have a lot of doctor and nurse friends, and I love them. I know they are doing the very best they can with what they have. But I just felt the lack of compassion and the ability to see me as a really scared woman who is having all of these crazy symptoms and no one is giving me a straight answer. I was seen as a 34-year-old female. I was a statistic. I was really angry at first, but I have had some time."

When I listen to this story, I think of the nurse who knew something was wrong (but whose hands were tied) as the glimmer of compassion in this narrative.

That nurse knew, but there was nothing she was *permitted* to do. This is a sticking point for me. What do we do? Where can we draw from when our inner knowing is clear but our environment is dismissive? What is available to us? At present, there seems to be a common theme in our world of constriction. I hear a lot of people say: "Well, if I was allowed, I'd be helpful."

Lisa's story seems to me a beacon of bringing more humanity into our medicine and remembering the power of human knowing. Where are the lines of personal responsibility to our family of humanity?

Plus, there is the balance of human knowing. In this case, the balance of knowing was skewed. Sometimes we come from a clear knowing, like Lisa did. Then other times we let our fear take over and tell us what we can and cannot do, or we let our beliefs blind our vision. In this story, I would assign that role to the attending doctors. Labels or externals do not compensate for internal knowing, for intuition. Yoga, although ancient, was seen as a peripheral new wave at one point, and now it has been accepted. There is actually a yogic science to being in balance and at ease in the human form.

I imagine how this life-changing experience has crafted Lisa as a yoga teacher. How does her experience inform her yogic space of body presence and embodiment?

"I try to hold space," she explains of her role as a yoga instructor. "I try to bring myself back. Over the years, I have been working on being a better listener. It's hard. I'm not the only one that struggles with that. But I try to bring myself back to those moments when I was literally just spoken over. They all kept saying: 'You're fine.' But deep down, I know I am not.

"Yoga was really the homerun for me. Because mind, body, and heart are one cohesive unit; when it works together, it is really beautiful. When you have a realization of all [of] them together and that they are working towards being a well-oiled machine, if you will, it's eye-opening.

"Drawing it back to the student who says, 'I don't think I can do this. I'm not strong or flexible enough.' Well, I'm like, 'Join the club.' I'm not that flexible either. But I want to hear what you really have to say, and why do you believe that? I think it's really important to see people, meet them where they are, and really hear them. Hearing them with an open mind and an open heart. Not just like, I have these preconceived notions of what they are going to say, keep a smile on your face, and fake it. But are you *really* hearing them? That is one of the things I have learned from all of this. At some point in our life, we have all been glossed over, if you will."

We *all* have been "glossed over" at some point. We have a choice to walk it differently—reclaim a bit of ourselves. I say to Lisa, "Even though our journeys are not the same, we come upon similar wisdom because we are all human. Without asking you to pinpoint one thing, may I ask you who you were after the stroke versus who you are now nine years later? What do you think are some of the things that pulled you up and out of that valley?"

"Right after my stroke was a very hard time for me. I always prided myself on being real gritty. I persevere. That's been, like, my thing. I was a swimmer in college, and I wasn't really good, but dammit if I wouldn't stay in the pool the entire practice, and if I had to do the entire set of 5,000 yards without stopping, I would do it. Because I wanted it. It was something I really loved, and I just, liked kind of being perceived as the underdog.

"What was hard for me, after my stroke..." She sighs deeply and begins again. "So one of my main issues now is that I have chronic pain. I was like, *I don't want to live like this.* Embarrassing is not the right word, but I was very shocked at how I felt like I was giving up—very easily.

"And so what kind of pulled me out was that I survived, right? Like, I made it. All of these things that happened, while at the moment I was angry, I knew in the long run, like whatever you believe in, God, the Universe, whatever your faith is—I have faith in God—I was like, *There's a reason that I survived.* And I held on to that. I didn't know what it was; I was literally in shock. But I knew there was a reason, and damn if I was not going to make it count. You know."

I do. There are these moments that we can feel the ease of sliding down, the mountain too great to climb. Then we remember that glimmer of: *This is my life, and I have to rise to that.*

The first thing Lisa needed was to understand her "new normal." She remembers being in the hospital when an occupational therapist (OT) came in to see how well she could maneuver in new situations. The OT was showing Lisa how to get in the shower, and Lisa was confused. I remember a similar confusion when a nurse told me to ring the bell for help to the bathroom after my emergency C-section. I was perplexed, just like Lisa remembers being. I didn't ring the bell. I pulled myself out of bed, and when I made a slight turn backwards, just like Lisa, I fell. I had not internalized the state my new body was in. The OT prompted Lisa, "That is not how you get into the shower now. That might be how you get in the shower in maybe ten months, but it's not how you are going to get into the shower right now. You're gonna put one foot in at a time."

It is quite surreal when your mind has a different perception than your body's reality. Lisa had this new question of: *How do I figure out how to make myself healthy again? How do I get into and establish this new normal?*

Her second benchmark was, how would she share this information? How could she share the meaning that she "drew from it, which is: No matter what life throws at you, don't give up. Keep being gritty. Action is sometimes gonna be messy, but just get in there and do it. Live," she says.

There is something deeply humbling for me when I hear someone who decides from a foundational place that life is worth it. It is always worth it. It gives me pause and a reason to rise again.

"For me, it was literally one breath at a time. My faith helped me know—it was a peace within that resided. *Oh, you're here. You survived. What are you going to do with this second chance?* I was like: 'I hear that loud and clear. I receive that.' And that's where I am now," Lisa gives us.

"Right after my stroke, I wanted to downplay everything. I had a level of embarrassment, although that word isn't the best. How did a stroke happen to a 34 year old? And how did nobody catch it for three days? And how is it that I cannot feel pain or temperature on the entire left side of my body? Like all of these, 'How is this? How is this? How is this?' And then the turning point of, 'This is what is. And this is something that is permanent.'

"I remember thinking, I am 34. *I either lay down and die or get up and live.* It took a while to get there, but I was like, 'I am 34. I can't give up now. C'mon. I have a life to live. It might look different than I envisioned, but it's still life. It's gonna be beautiful at times. And ugly at times. And it's gonna be in the middle too. But don't give up.' That is one of the things I kept telling myself. It's not for anybody else, it's for me. It took that for me to realize—oh yeah, this life is for me.

"I still struggle with that idea of what people think of me, or how I come across. Am I too much? Am I not enough? Do I say too much? Do I say not enough? But at the end of the day, I know it's for me. What happened to me is maybe different than what happened to you, but at the end of the day, we're here. We didn't give up.

"So just keep truckin'. Keep moving forwards, because if you don't, you're going backwards... or standing still. Life is uncomfortable. But I believe in myself so much that I believe in you—and everyone else."

That's the power of belief. It is contagious and inexhaustible. The more it is given, the more it grows. No matter how varied the stories, these glimmers of human existence come through. Some stories, like Lisa's, shine so bright from her committed grace that she has light to share. Illumination to give. I believe that that glimmer of human existence is really the fabric of our divinity. Lisa reminds us—lest we forget— about the way life carries on. It's designed to. Your life is designed *for* you. You are designed to meet and alchemize all that arises on your path. Sometimes you have the tools; sometimes the obstacles appear so you can gain new ones. Sometimes a twist turns us towards an innocence or a bravery that waited for this moment to bloom.

Your life is designed for you.

In a rebirth, we can be humbled back to our core, where we rediscover the tenacity, curiosity, and faith of our essence waiting to serve us.

We may forget our inner knowing, yet it leaves us not. We may not find ourselves easily meeting the mettle of life with magic, yet we will carry on.

It's okay to believe in miracles. It's okay to believe in yourself no matter what your path looks like right now. The path, as Lisa reminds us, is one that we *get to walk*. She prompts us to look at the source inside to become better listeners to our own voice, and to learn how to be heard. First by our own selves and then by the world that holds us as we dance through this life, aligned body, mind, and soul.

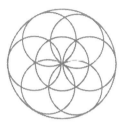

Continuous Becoming

I first heard of Kim Murriera at a beach potluck on the East Side of Kauai. I was looking for a new rental as an outsider in a close-knit community. A friend of a friend said they knew Kim had a room, and she assured me she would pass along the contact information as we dipped into a bowl of freshly made guacamole with the waves of Kealia landing behind us. I had recently returned from a trip to Peru after only moving to Kauai a few months earlier to find my once-quiet sublet had taken a deleterious turn such that the landlord humbly offered to release me from my lease. I thanked him for his kindness and set to work to find a new space. In the interim, I took a month-to-month sublet. By the time the beach potluck contact details arrived, they also came with the disclaimer that the room for rent had already been filled.

I still called. I had made a promise to myself and the Universe: I promised that I would call *every* reliable lead that came my way, and in turn I would trust that I'd find my room by my December deadline. I left Kim a voicemail.

A week later, Kim called back and said the room had unexpectedly opened. She had previously settled on a tenant that was disruptive, and he had to leave—was I still interested?

I went to this little jungle bungalow and was blown away by the magic of open land. The purples and greens of lush beauty inside and outside of the house were heart opening. As soon as I met Kim and stood inside the hale (house), I knew this was my new home. I didn't know that I would be meeting a deeply wise, playful master teacher who would also become a beloved lifelong friend.

Sometimes the most necessary action is a leap of trust. Florence Scovel Shinn says, "Never violate a hunch." Often life's treasures are waiting on the other side of our faith in ourselves. That kind of trust threads through Kim Murriera's life and artistry. Known in her circle of friends and students as a gifted storyteller, artist, and guide, Kim uses presence and practice to bring one back to the body's and the heart's deep knowing. She is comfortable knowing that as much as she teaches, she learns. And as much as she grows, she is continuously becoming.

Meet Kim Murriera

To understand Kim Murriera's new beginning, we need to understand where she rebirthed from. Kim's roles and training include: creative arts therapist, biographical practitioner, and Waldorf teacher, who founded and ran a Waldorf-inspired school on the island of Kauai for eight years. When you walk into Kim's studio, mosaiced and nuanced, surrounded by verdant Kauai beauty and the song of the shama birds, her titles of artist and "Midwife of the Creative" truly land.

She trained in child development in California, earning her teaching certificate at Emerson College in the UK for Waldorf/Steiner Education. Teaching children for 23 years, her understanding of child development, human consciousness, and the medicine of the creative—for all ages—to integrate and unfurl inner knowing is wide and deep. Make yourself a cup of tea; our journey through the cycles and wisdom of rebirth are turning towards the subtlety of spirit.

Her studio defies the muted, drab concrete classrooms of my youth, with their old bulletin boards trimmed with last year's staples. When I stood in her classroom with art all about on the colored walls and a candle lit, watching with rapt attention as children sat in wooden chairs, surrounded by jingles and jangles of beauty, I not only felt awe, but grief. I had no idea education could look like this. No cold chairs or lined formations. Rather, children were spiraled: seated organically at elongated, communal tables, encouraged to help each other with a teacher guiding and pushing (my word, not Kim's) the children to new horizons. I accepted that ardent structure is necessary—and make no mistake, there is structure and expectation in Kim's classroom—but the tools to reach the same end of structure and discipline invite the whole child, not just a demand for performance.

When Kim first encountered Waldorf Education, she had never before met a form of child development that went as deep. "I could spend lifetimes and still not get to the bottom of the well of the wisdom. Whether Waldorf is right for every child in the world is another discussion," Kim drops right in.

I loved school as a child, and I had the grace of amazing teachers, which along with my mother's ardent support of education, built the entree to my decade as a public educator. I aimed to bring life and learning to my students, but I was absolutely shocked to see how much more was possible, and how much already existed in a very different experience of education.

> "Holistic education is a term that is thrown around a lot these days. It is an interesting thing for me to watch and wonder: *Do we really know what that means when we say it?*" Kim asks.

> "If we look at the human body, there are the arms and the feet, which are the will—our doing in the world. It is how we go out and accomplish things. There is the torso, which houses the rhythmic system—the heart. I like to explain that as the 'feeling' life because the heart is there," she says, her hands demonstrating. "And then there is the head on the human being, and that is the thinking—because the brain is there. If we are truly educating the whole human being, and we are looking at the human being, we need to be speaking to the will (the doing); the heart (the feeling); and we need to activate the mind (the thinking). If we

are not doing all of those at the same time, in every lesson, in every class, in every theme, in every year, then we're not truly educating in a holistic way with children... or adults."

The concept of addressing the whole being so thoroughly may sound novel and unrealistic—I know it did to me until I experienced it. The truth does not need us to acknowledge it for it to exist, yet when we do, opportunities abound. As a human family, we agree that children need to be treated with great care, but *are* they treated with great care? Do we respect their need for slow, soft, and sweet integration against the pace of the modern world? If adults in an art room look forlornly at children's playful drawings and holistically-held nurturance, maybe we could do a better job honoring our children and their pace, and consequently ourselves.

As we delve into Kim's world, let's leave a door open for this contemplation, for with each rebirth, that which was unattended arises for integration. Let me say that again:

For each turn around the spiral, with each birth or rebirth, that which was previously unattended arises to be integrated.

It seems to be the brilliance in the design of life's wisdom. Slowing down to give yourself space to witness without expectation can be powerful. Let us create room for this contemplation that education and understanding of our human experience, especially for our children, can be different.

"The reason why I moved from children to adults is when adults came into my classroom at night for art class, and they'd see the stuff hanging from the kids and hear me talk about it, they would say, 'We want you to teach us like you teach the children,'" Kim says.

"Can you tell us more about Waldorf? Not everyone understands it," I offer.

"I often hear," Kim sighs, "'Oh, that is the school that does art.' Well it is, and it's really important to me to correct that. Yes, Waldorf is the school that does the art, but we're not the school that you *go* to [for] an art class. We are the educational system and curriculum that uses art to illuminate knowledge. And when you do that—it sticks. Because you have awakened a feeling to it.

"But," Kim's voice lilts, "it does mean you need to slow it down. In our fast-paced society, where we want more, more, more, it can trigger some people into thinking they are not getting enough, and it's a hard thing in our times to have people open to an embodied and ensouled experience. When it happens, we walk away remembering it. In the West, with more and more technology, we are leaning towards primarily educating the mind, and that's lovely. I absolutely think we should be using our minds. I am not in an Eastern focus where I feel like we should always be getting rid of the mind, but if we are only educating the mind, we do not walk away feeling enriched and given something that nourishes us. Oftentimes we can feel depleted if we are fed only in the mind," Kim explains.

Expansion and contraction are intimate partners in our mind's growth. To that end, I ask Kim, "Was it an easy decision to stop teaching kids?"

"It is a hard world to leave," she answers honestly. "Because teaching children and Waldorf education is so near and dear to my heart, and even though there is so much I could say about it, it really wasn't right for me anymore. It took a lot of courage, and something that comes with age and experience—the will to stand up in the knowing when life is asking me to turn in another direction. It's not an easy thing to do and trust, but there was really no other option for me at that point. My body wouldn't let me teach anymore."

It is tricky for us humans when impending change is true and clear yet still difficult to accept. We could be fighting the idea that we deserve better, that we are one of the ones it all works out for. We could be so busy wrestling with time and the concept of linear success that we time out of the chance for wild leaps and radical change. These questions create the perfect darkness for doubt to grow. Especially (and we saw this in Christina Super Friedland's story, too) when you are already doing something that is serving others and the outside perception is that you should stay where you are, it can be really hard to leave.

> Kim confirms, "I had a lot of doubt, and I held onto it for too long. If I am not really responding to what I know to be true internally, then the Universe, life, whatever you want to call it, will just take me and place me somewhere else. I call these destiny moments," Kim says. "We can show up for them or not, but again, sometimes life will create a situation where what needs to end... ends."

The ending created and recreated itself for Kim. She kept trying to carry on operating the school. She tried to train two different teachers, but both fell through abruptly. Loyal and true, she then tried to find another location—a satellite school to place her families in—and that didn't work.

The more she tried, the more precarious the circumstances became until the moment she let go.

She realized that it was best for herself and her students to let go. Even when we may love and enjoy something, roles and circumstances can call for change. As Kim says, destiny is waiting. The new cycle is starting—with or without your consent.

While this change was coming to fruition, Kim concurrently birthed *Create Yourself Awake*, a six-month creative arts journey for adults. Knowing that she would be transitioning completely to adult education, she knew there was another piece to the puzzle. There was a body of work that was calling, which had intrigued her as a twenty-something studying at Emerson. She decided this was the moment. Kim calls it "a four-month break from my life." Her "break" entailed: arranging the caretaking of her land, renting out her home and studio, and independently sourcing new income for six months (including creating and selling her first pieces of fine art) while paying to travel and apprentice in a new body of work. I'd sooner call it a grand leap of faith than a break.

"What was the work you were going to study?" I ask.

> "It's called biography counseling, a Rudolph Steiner based work that is still taught at Emerson, where I did my original training. This work," Kim explains, "looks at people's stories (biographies) in a very intimately holistic and spiritual perspective."

She would apprentice with Ilena Botero, who taught at the Center for Social Development, an offshoot of Emerson, many years ago. Then, the biography work was the main focus of the school. Botero, born a Columbian, settled in Forest Row, England in her early years. Decades later, a friend of Kim's, Annie, approached the master teacher and said, "I know this friend that really wants to learn this work and wondered if you would do a custom training for her?"

Annie went on and on, so the story goes, about Kim's creations and accomplishments, professionally and personally—a "true cheerleader," Kim chuckles.

Months later, Kim arrived—in every sense—in front of her teacher. Kim and Ilena were sitting face to face, acknowledging all that needed to happen to create this moment together, when her teacher said, "You know, when Annie came to me and was going on and on about all of your accomplishments, internally I was rolling my eyes. I don't often say yes, but at the very end of Annie's monologue, she took a breath and said, 'She's going to have to work really hard to get here, and it is that important to her.'

"That's the moment I said yes," Ileana said. "I wanted to meet your striving."

> "It silenced me," Kim's voice wanders. "If it had been easy for me to fly over, Kate, it might not have happened. I had to want it that badly. I needed to rise, and in my rising, or striving, she came forward."

So much of modern learning is seen as a reciprocal, linear endeavor. I give x and get y in return. I invest enough money and I get the accreditation I desire. Apprenticeships such as the one Kim entered into are rare—or rarely spoken of. When you embark on a new journey, unconventional opportunities or mentors may come to you (if you are available)—this is the good stuff. The really good stuff. But you must slow down and have the courage and the humility to meet it. It can feel scary to only have the confirmation of your own knowing.

I remember having a candid talk with Kim about how she was ever going to finance this trip on a zoom call. She was in her studio, surrounded by art and beauty, creations by herself and her students. I, in an old, three-story row house in Philadelphia, PA with cars careening outside my window. I asked if she would ever consider making art to sell.

"Oh, I don't do that," she said.

Don't we all do that? Say, *I don't do that.* Haven't we all said, *Oh, the thing that brings me innate joy—that? Use that to sustain me? Who would want that? Why would I do that?* But then we do it, and a new freedom evolves. It can be a subtle twist amidst a large shift, or it can be the shift itself.

The simple support of someone else seeing you can often show—well, I used to say it shows—what we cannot see. But now I think that if you have a true friend reflect an insight to you, they reflect what we are ready to see in ourselves. Sometimes it is in the container of reflection that we can hear our own clarity. That is the nature of our interconnectedness as part of this human family.

> In her biography client work, Kim "stands witness and brings forward the stories of your life. We tangibly write them down," she explains. "To see patterns, see mirroring moments, see planetary moments. But one of my jobs as the person that is accompanying you on this journey is to help with the telling; typically, when we are telling a story in life, we go to [where] the trauma hit, where it was painful, when we retell the story.

"We can be in a pattern of retelling the story in the same way, over and over again. One of my jobs is to help broaden and contextualize the events. While being a skillful question asker, I am helping you bring out the whole context of the story: Where was it located? Was it sunrise or sunset? Were there flowers blooming? Was there another person there? What else happened in that week? Who was the helper that you didn't even know? So that you begin to see it in a holistic environment," Kim gently invites.

"Yes, we were hit by a trauma," she continues. "Yes, it affected us in a particular way. I had a client who one of the major events in her life was a car crash when she was very little in which her whole family was in the car. As we were exploring that moment, she said at one point, 'I went back to the car crash and raised above it and saw that there was a beautiful sky in the background, and that there were people coming to help us.' She pulled back from the event and saw that it was a beautiful day, and people were running to help them. It's work where we start to rearrange how we are relating to life and see it in a broader view to give you a bird's eye perspective on your own life."

"Does that scare some people?" I ask.

"Oh yeah," Kim answers easily. "They're terrified. I have people slinking through the door. Life is confronting. There is a phrase in the biographical world: 'Your life is your dignity.'"

She confides, "I watch people's faces when I say that, and often they will pause and say: 'What does that really mean?' I had that happen in my six-month course recently, and I asked the woman: 'Well, what does that mean to you?'And she answered, 'I am not really sure.'

"So I asked her, 'Are there any moments in your life where you put your head down when you are talking about them?'" Kim asked. "'Oh, yeah,' the woman said.

"Well, that's what I am talking about. I want us to be able to rise and our shoulders to go back and down. I want our eyes to soften, and I want to be able to speak those stories without a constriction in the throat. And to rise into the dignity of all of our lives— not just our accomplishments."

Honestly, when I listened to this segment of our chat while editing this book, I felt a constriction because I perceived myself as living one of those phases recently, where I was unable to embrace all that was. So how dare I share these stories? Yet the very stories I felt momentarily unworthy to carry were the bearers of the medicine I needed to recalibrate how I perceived myself.

Your life is your dignity.

That is what I mean by life's spiral and the misnomer of linearity. Was I lost? Or was I diving deeper—and honestly, does it feel any different in the moment? I had so many people cheering me on, yet all I saw were the places that did not go to plan. Full stop. With time, I allowed myself to see what was happening holistically, and my perspective changed. The constriction fell away. We can have contradictions where we are thriving and failing simultaneously. I don't know *how* this is so, I just know it is. Walt Whitman says it beautifully: "Do I contradict myself? Very well then I contradict myself. I am large. I contain multitudes."

My life had left the known and spiraled into the unknown, yet from a bird's eye perspective, I had everything I needed, and I was learning to create a sense of sovereignty and self-reliance, the depths of which I never would have reached without living through uncertainty. Every so often, I am reminded that there is not a timeline to the ups and downs of life's ferris wheel. Life goes round and round, and when it is your turn to be tossed about—to take a phrase from Kim—expand your vision to include the seen and unseen hands arranging the moment. You may be shocked if you let yourself be loved by life.

I ask Kim: "What are some of the things that help people reclaim that dignity?"

> "Working with someone consistently over a long time, we allow someone their own unfolding," Kim expounds. "Similar to a flower in the plant kingdom. If we are watching those time-lapse videos, and they speed it up, we are like, wow! But in real time, you would have to be sitting next to the flower 24 hours a day for a few days to watch it unfold; honestly, you wouldn't probably notice it until it has unfolded.

> "In a fast-paced time of sound bytes, memes, and two-minute videos, we want things that fast. Now, I know I am a Taurus, and I move slowly, but in my experience, healing and perspective take time. In my work, I am educating your perspective muscles so that you begin to change how you see your life and other. Biography work is about Spirit, self, and other. That takes time—to change habits, to see life differently, to strengthen that muscle of perception, so that we can see self and other in a different way.

> "My favorite work is in groups," she shares. "When I am working with a biography group, and we are hearing other people's stories, it contextualizes our own life. When you hear that someone's overarching theme matches your own, it helps you to realize life is not all about me and my traumas. We all have them. Life is cyclic, and that is what I like to illuminate. There is a breathing in and a breathing out. There is a waning and waxing. There is happiness and there is sadness. And of course, as we grow and get older and gather tools, we are able to keep our equanimity more, but it doesn't change the duality of life. It is our *relationship* to that duality that can change."

Rebirth, podcast and book, stands on these same pillars of belief. It started as sharing a collection of stories of women I knew doing marvelous things because there is wisdom for us in witnessing the stories of others, in seeing yourself in others. It takes us out of isolation into activation—that this is life, and you are perfectly designed to live yours. There are tools. There are ways. There is help, within and without, to go where your inner star is pointing. When you hear the mirrored theme of another's life, you are reminded that you are indeed not alone, and this cycle, as Kim says, will not last forever, yet there is great medicine to be had here.

> "I also teach Steiner's view of human development," Kim continues. "If we get *any* development education, it is about children's development, zero to seven or seven to fourteen, but I love teaching the deep wisdom, otherworldly view on the unfoldment of the whole human being. When we contextualize life in that way, we can see that there are themes. There are things coming. There is a contraction and expansion in life, there are cycles. It lets us rest in that dignity more. We may realize, *It's not just me and my life; it's how life is.* We can settle into breathing into it with more calm and vitality and acceptance."

So what do we do? Many of us were not told about these natural cycles and patterns of life that continue through our adulthood and beyond, or that there is a season of growth that continuously expands as we age. We were only told we could rent a car at 25 years of age—and off we go!

> "To see the truth," Kim continues, "we must first imagine the whole. If we can reach back into our past, when we hear about human development, and also reach into our future, which is not a fixed box, destiny is then dynamic and unpredictable, which is wonderful. There are themes that we can rest into. A container that can hold us for growing through this life. When we can get an imagination, it leaves room—there is more truth that can come forward."

"And what does that mean for us?" I ask.

"We are surrounded by natural cycles, and I like to ground into those more and more. I often have parents call me and say: 'I put my child in a new school and they are struggling,'" she explains. "And I ask, 'How many weeks has it been?' And they say, 'A week.' I tell them not to make any decisions until the child goes through a full moon cycle (new to full, 28 days). You have to allow the expansion and contraction to see where we are really at. Until you ride that wave all the way through, it's hard to get a clear picture.

"In *Create Yourself Awake*, my six-month course on creativity, I start off with a lens into the creative process," she explains. "I do that through an Eastern perspective of the five elements: Fire, Air, Water, Earth, and Ether. Each element represents an aspect of the creative journey. What I am trying to illuminate is the importance of starting somewhere in the cycle of elements. You can start with the spark of an idea (fire), or you can begin with working a medium (water) and then move from that point. You can start with any element. What matters is that you start and allow the cycle/circle to continue.

"The cycle doesn't end, and when you understand each of the elements in the process, you become aware when you hit one which is weak for you. We all have one that is unfamiliar or difficult for us, and this is when you usually walk away. If you understand that is where you get stuck, but there is more on the other side to carry you through, then you can breathe through it, trust, and keep going."

So let's walk through that again. You may be someone who loves to get up and go, so when it comes time to sit and settle inward, you hit a place of discomfort because it is not your default. If you stay, you get the freedom of moving through what you believed you could not accomplish. As for the concepts of elements, they pertain to form and a feeling as well. Let yourself lean into the textured, substantive difference between air and water, fire and earth, and you can start to expand into Kim's invitation.

> "In the biography work," Kim continues, "Steiner views human development through seven-year cycles, and each seven-year cycle is ruled by a planet... By the way, you don't have to understand or believe in that to engage in the work. I hold that space for you— but each of those seven-year cycles is maturing an organ of perception. How I translate that: The human being is unfinished," Kim says.

> "It's not like we turn 18 and we have all our stuff together. We are of age, but there are things we are still learning. We are still maturing certain perceptions in our seventies and in our eighties, and each one builds onto the next one. It anchors us in. It's not that I arrive somewhere. It's that I am building and fortifying a maturity in life that is continuous and never-ending, much like the growth of a tree."

I don't know about you, but I fully bought into the idea of arriving in my thirties, or so I thought. Then it sneakily reared its head again in my forties, and I have been having to disassemble, brick by brick, the idea of arriving and expanding into the gracious expansion of continuous growth. I have also started to turn towards the need for being and offering what I have learned. It is one way we can give back—or more aptly, forward—for the bounties we have received in our lives. The gems we have been given or hewn over time. As an elder friend of mine shares, "It's our rent for getting to live here on Earth."

Another close friend, this one in his thirties, confided in me that since he was happily married and had arrived at success professionally, he didn't want for much and enjoyed the life he had. After a few accomplishments, he kind of wondered what the point of his later years were going to be. I told him, "Just because society has sold us on doing, don't be fooled by the preciousness of being and the necessity of eldership—in all forms. Not just your children (he had none), but nieces and nephews, or those that life will place in front of you. That is desperately needed now and always will be."

We don't know where life is heading, but I am certain it is not linear. As Kim says, it is cyclic. We can be at once learning and helping others learn. We can be lost and found. We don't know what is in store for us around the next turn of the spiral. Best to stay curious. We don't know who we are here to serve, so stay open.

When I sit with what I have learned from Kim, from Steiner's philosophies, and other interconnected philosophies, it is quite laughable that we hand a piece of paper to an 18 year old and ask them what they are going to be. Perhaps, with a small shift, we could ask our liminal adults, "What more would you like to learn? What would you like to teach one day?" I wonder if that small shift of expansion and interconnection might not change how we feel about the unavoidable peaks and valleys across our lifetime.

Kim offered us this parting gift: "When I was in my twenties, one [of] my then teachers told me: 'One of the worst things we can ever do to a human being is believe that they cannot change.'"

We can change. What we do, where we live, who we serve can all change. Who we love can change, and it doesn't have to be an *either/or*. It may very well be an *and*. We cannot stop the infinite, so why not embrace the contradictory multitude life offers us?

There was no logical reason that on a windy beach on the East side of Kauai, one new acquaintance would know a friend that would lead to an apparent dead end that opened me up to a new home and a whole new family of community (a story for another time). What unseen hands were at work then?

When we leave room at our table for the unknown, we create a chance for inspired expansion. We alert the mentors, the serendipities, and the destiny moments waiting in the wings that they are indeed welcome. We may even assume dignity in our lives, no longer burdened by the thought that we are only our accomplishments, but rather the alchemy of our flaws, our chances taken, our perspectives gained, and our life lived. What a wonderful truth to carry with us: *The human being is unfinished.* You are unfinished, continuously becoming. How infinitely beautiful is that?

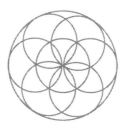

Trust Your Place

I am a huge dog lover. Everything about them: their paws and noses, their sense of the pack and loyalty, the way in which they move about the world, imprinting compassion and hopefulness. I know so many other animals are fancier, but there is nothing more humbling than unconditional love, and dogs have that to spare. Part of that is because they understand their place in the pack. It could be seen as diminutive, but in the natural order of things, when you know your purpose (your place), incredible freedom ensues.

So when I came home one day, years ago, and my then roommate suggested that we get a dog as a deterrent to a small outbreak of crime in our rural neighborhood, I think it surprised her when I said no. Absolutely not.

"But why?"

"Because, I cannot 'sort of' have a dog." I shrug after my air quotes. See, some people can. They can, for the benefit of both the human and the dog, let the dog be. Maybe the dog lives outside, or it has a nice kennel in the living room. That is not me. When I have a dog, we merge. They become an equal member in my life, and that's just the way it is. If you meet my dog, you'd understand as she blinks at you from the passenger seat of the car, head cocked to the side, or more accurately, gaze settled on the horizon.

I didn't want a dog because I was traveling a lot and planned to travel more. One reason I was traveling so much was that I was free to: My very best friend, who had also lived on four paws, had passed only six months earlier, so there was absolutely no way I was ready for another fur friend. It would be unfair because no dog could live up to Kyla.

"But we could let this dog live outside." My roommate offered a logical solution in a tropical climate with a house that had a wraparound porch.

"No way, I couldn't do it," I answered, knowing myself way too well.

About a week later, two different friends forwarded me the same email from the Humane Society stating that there was an emergency foster situation; they had rescued a house full of dogs, and their kennels were in overflow. They needed help rehabilitating some pups until there was more room in the kennels. *This*, I thought, *could be right up my alley*.

Here was my thinking: I would rehab a dog for a few weeks and know that it was just for convalescence. That way I would have boundaries, my roommate could have a dog's presence, and I could do a mitzvah (good deed) in the process. The only official mitzvah I have ever done was when I met up with my college boyfriend's mother and her synagogue to walk greyhounds. When I tell you dogs are my people, I mean it.

I drove down to the Humane Society where my friend was working, and I walked in, asking her, "Where are the kennels?"

"Your dog is this way," she answered.

"Pam," I corrected her, "I'm not adopting."

"Oh, I know," she called over her shoulder.

I walked down the hallway, flip flops echoing into my friend's office, where a black dog with one white paw and a tan collar sat, a bit too perfectly, obviously aware of the plan.

"This is Tawny."

"Tawny?" I scrunched my face. The dog was obviously too magnificent for such a name. Also, her fur was black.

"Yes. She is a doll. I love having her in the office—you will love her."

"I'm not adopting."

"Oh, I know, I know," my friend said, gathering a leash and what-not.

"What about her vest?" The Humane Society had a program where foster dogs were given vests so that when you had them out and about, if someone fell in love, it would increase the chances of adoption.

"Oh, you know, it's so hot, and she has black fur." My friend avoided eye contact with me. "She doesn't need one."

"I'm not adopting, Pam."

"Oh, I know. I know."

She walked us out to the car a few minutes later, and as I was helping soon-not-to-be-Tawny into my tan-interior Mazda, I turned to wave good-bye to my friend. She waved and smiled. With not one letter of exaggeration, she turned and clicked her heels in triumph, and part of me started to realize something else was afoot.

I had happened, before driving down to the Humane Society, to pop open the ʻŌlelo Noʻeau by Mary Kawena Pukui, a book of Hawaiian proverbs, to spot pick a name. You know, when you close your eyes, flip open a page, point your finger, then open your eyes. This is what I read: Ahonui. It can translate to "patience with perseverance."

It would take seven days before I would drive back down to the Humane Society, pluck Tawny's photo off the adoption board, and make it official. It would take a few more weeks before I would open my heart. We got her an indoor bed and a raised outdoor bed. She would sleep on the porch right by my bedroom window. I would wake up and see her eyes peering at me from the outside. I would let her in and do all the dog things: walk her, love her up, help her acclimate. But it was weeks after that, when one morning (she had started sleeping inside, in her dog bed at the foot of my bed) I looked at her and she held my stare. She held my stare and said: *You are going to love me, and I can wait.*

I literally felt my heart burst open for this boundless pup. She was undeterred by my resistance because she understood her place and our destiny. When you hear things like *be here now*, this is what that looks like. Don't turn away from the very real love that awaits you—whether that be a pup, a person, or a calling—because of what once was. In this case, grief was halting my joy. Other common culprits are: doubt, unworthiness, martyrdom—you get the idea. I love the story of how Ahonui arrived into my life because it is how she lives: lovingly. She has gone on to travel back and forth across the country with me, helping me in teacher trainings, client sessions, personal adventures, and even acclimating to parenting. All of this love was destined.

That which is for you cannot be taken away from you, but I'll say for myself, it can sometimes be slowed down a little by my own resistance. I wish I could say that resisting the love and generosity that was waiting for me in Ahonui's arrival was anomalous in my evolution. However, I *am* getting better every day. Some people are inherently more at ease with transition and the changes that life offers. They know when to flow and listen, like David Newman.

Meet David Newman

Some of us quiver at the thought of a new sojourn; others have a travel bag packed for when life calls. David Newman is a renowned sacred mantra artist, singer-songwriter, and inspirational teacher. David opened a yoga studio in Philadelphia decades before yoga studios and coffee shops were on every corner. In fact, it is where I learned yoga training and taught yoga for several years. David sold the studio over a year before we chatted on Rebirth, but it was a cornerstone of the Philadelphia yoga community for 27 years, and when he began to walk another artery of the yogic path the studio was booming.

"David, could you walk us through why opening Yoga on Main was such a big leap?"

> "Absolutely," he offers. "In the early 1990s, I was in law school in New York City, and I stumbled upon a yogi in New York who was living in Maui at the time. I went to his weekend workshop, and I was absolutely blown away. My second year of law school, I became impassioned, almost obsessed with yoga. I basically studied my law courses and practiced yoga for hours a day. That was life.

> "In 1992," he continues, "I moved from New York back home to Philadelphia with this law degree, but also this extraordinary interest and desire to teach yoga, and got the blessing of this particular teacher," David adds.

Since yoga is a tradition, it is often not enough to attend training. To teach with authenticity, there needs to be permission from the teacher, similar to Kim Murriera's apprenticeship for her work at Emerson. David was sitting between the crossroads of a very traditional education and an ancient one as both lawyer and yogi.

> "After taking the bar exam in August, I figured, just for—" his voice pauses. "I wouldn't say for the fun of it because I was deeply inspired. But I thought, *I'll look for some real estate spaces.* So I drove around and found this space in a little town outside center city in Manayunk with a *For Rent* sign, and I saw the yoga center that was to be there."

"That's amazing," I replied.

"And I never turned back. My parents, who are more professionally oriented, thought I would get it out of my system," David says. "But that never came to pass. Now it is more deeply in my system."

I can't help but ask him what he thought of the law school experience in relation to where he is now. David shares that while he was in his third year of law school, he journeyed to upstate New York with a dear friend who was studying with a Lakota medicine man, Izzy Heartman Zaphirto. Near the end of the sweat lodge, Izzy shared a channeled message from Grandfather Spirit for everyone in the sweat lodge. The message that came through for David was: "One day you will be an advocate for me."

"And for those that know law," David expands, "know that is what it is called: You are *advocating* for your client."

One of David's gifts is holding space in the moment. I have witnessed it over the years, and I am not surprised at his composure and presence, even though he is the one being interviewed. With his chestnut eyes and soft composure, he lets you know he is fully present while maintaining a firm clarity of his own knowing. Messaging, movement, and heeding wisdom are consistent threads running through David's story. It is a part of the magic he offers. With his way of showing up and putting in the effort yet holding the mantle of the world loosely so when it comes time to change, he appears to walk onward in that direction with a certitude I admire.

> "So over the years, my capacity to communicate and clarify my thoughts as a teacher were deeply shaped by law school. I share in ways that can be received and digested meaningfully to people," David connects.

David goes on to draw another comparison of how law school also developed yogic tools and perspective: the ability to "suspend judgment" and see a problem, even advocate for or against something from all sides. David clarifies that it is even a form of discipline:

> "In law school, you get a case, and rather than advocate for this person or that person, you look into how all the possible sides would advocate their case, so it gives you the capacity to step back and understand, objectively observe the situation, and make

arguments from all perspectives. That is very yogic—the ability to read a situation with an open mind. And that has stayed with me in my yoga practice and my approach to life."

"That's beautiful," I respond. "I think when we are in the middle of something, it can sometimes be hard to see how it all weaves together. But with time and perspective, we can see life's tapestry."

"Yes," David says. "Suspending judgment. And I think you get a clearer picture of a situation when you don't just jump into it. You watch and wait and look, and that requires a certain kind of discipline. I feel that the beginnings of that discipline began in law school."

I love the word discipline. I have reworked my relationship to it. I grew up (as I have learned) in a supportive and structured environment. I think in many ways, it served me and my personality well. Attending Catholic school, you learn a lot about discipline and paying attention to the fine lines of things. This is neither inherently good nor bad; it can be helpful when applied correctly. For instance, I am great with manners and demonstrating respect to those in power. My book covers and report covers were impeccable. I am still a bit of a mess, so I don't have that superb organization, but I did have a particular attention to rules that needed (in my best interest) to be softened a bit by life. I think that is why that one Sunday out of so many Sundays, when I was actually attending one of David's yoga classes, waiting for him to arrive, made such a deep impression.

"I remember being in one of your yoga classes—could have been for teacher training, I cannot recall," I begin. "But it was Sunday mornings…"

"Yes," David says. "Sunday mornings."

"And, I don't mean to put you on the spot, because it is a fabulous story," I start with my disclaimer, "but you were a little late to class because you were chanting. And you had just realized you were *going* to be chanting. There was something in this time period about you going from primarily teaching asana (yoga poses) to chanting. I mention the lateness because I remember your exuberance."

David laughs.

"You came onto the teacher's platform and so happily said, 'Guys, wait until you hear what I have to share with you,'" I reminisce enthusiastically.

David laughs more.

"To me," I continue, "that was authenticity. I don't think I can remember any other class as clearly as I can remember your exuberance that day."

I know it is poor form to draw attention to what may be perceived as a snafu when you are playfully interviewing someone for a podcast, but you know what happened when he told his class? We loved it. We were overjoyed for him because it was real. To me, it was a brilliant display of someone aligned—a concept I was learning in a whole new way, to be aligned from inside out. Here was the head teacher, late to his own class because he was aligned with his own truth, and through his transparency, he invited us to the same.

If David was known to be tardy, would this be as significant? No. Is he often tardy? I don't know. I do know I took a bunch of his classes and studied yoga at his center, and "tardy" is not one of the first ten words I would use to describe him.

There is a great practice in being attentive and disciplined. I mentioned that I reworked my relationship to the word discipline, and although it would really blossom later, there were moments at Yoga on Main that the consideration of outside rules and perspectives being the only ones were becoming flimsy. The invitation to step a little deeper into life's spiral is a step towards the discipline of uplifting and nourishing your purpose through your unwavering commitment to it, to yourself, to your sovereignty—even if you aren't sure what that means yet. It's not all or nothing. It's an overflow of a thousand little moments like that one Sunday morning in David's class.

"I remember that actually," David chuckles. "I have always been grateful for the gift to be able to follow that enthusiasm, that inspiration, and to trust it even when it looks absurd.

"I'll tell you, Kate," he continues, "now there are yoga centers—even though many are closing—on every block in Philadelphia. In 1992, there weren't any yoga studios, and people around me thought it was absurd that I could even make a living off of a center that was devoted solely to the practice of yoga. Similarly, some years later, I really wanted to go more deeply into yoga practice, and I really thought it was going to be through the asana (physical) practice. And [then] I was introduced to chanting (kirtan)—and I had been a guitar player and songwriter literally since I was 13 years old. When I heard yoga come alive in sound and music through this practice of kirtan chanting, a light went off inside and said: 'Hey!' It was like meeting the person of your dreams. Everything I ever yearned for came together in one experience.

"So I started introducing chanting into my yoga classes," David expounds. "And when I first started doing it, I would begin class with a chant, which was new to everyone in my classes. People would sit on their pillows with their arms crossed and their lips sealed, like: *What is this? This is just bizarre.*"

David and I both laugh at the retelling because to date, he has 12 CDs and has toured internationally singing kirtan, and he successfully teaches others to sing and lead kirtan through his Kirtan College.

"Then a year later," David continues, "I came into class and said, 'Well, today, actually we're not going to chant, we're going to do a quiet meditation.' And everybody revolted: 'Whaddya mean we're not going to chant?'"

Again, David and I laugh. Humans are so funny when it comes to change and expectations.

"It was just my dharma or guidance to bring these mantras to people's attention," David says. "What happened for me was as I was teaching yoga classes, the initial chant that started class began as two minutes, then grew to five, ten, and around fifteen minutes, which is when I began to wonder if there was a career change calling me."

I love stories where you can hear the cadence of clarity that people allow and trust to guide them, and off they go. Also, seeing that it can happen more than once in a lifetime—we don't only get one shot.

This book is full of stories that debunk the heavily rotated myth that the likelihood of your failing is higher than the actuality that life is waiting for you to fly.

Taking in stories of faith and positivity feed our own optimism and attune your mindset, aligning you with the frequency of that which you are looking to create while helping to buoy your flow-state of faith.

"One thing about yogic spaces," I offer, "is that it can hold you really tightly, like Yoga on Main held many, and it can simultaneously teach you to not be attached."

"Absolutely," David agrees. "My favorite yoga story was by a teacher, Jiddhu Krishna Murti. Someone asked him once, 'Do you practice yoga?' And his answer was, 'Yes, but I try not to make a habit out of it.'"

David's transition from teaching physical practice to becoming an international kirtan performer and teacher happened over time. Eventually, his calling pulled him out of the studio he birthed. He entrusted Yoga on Main to his friend and studio manager, Shiva Das. Just like the pivot from law school, David heeded life's call to another turn.

"I am very guided on the inner planes, often through dreams," David states. "And I had a dream one night, and I heard this voice say, 'You are going to be asked to *go*, and when you are, *go*.' And that was the message I got, and my life just moved in a different direction. I found myself literally traveling all over the world until these last few months," David says, referring to 2020.

David and I chat about how his transition to teaching online shifted from a focus of performing with bands to educating others. He says, "I feel like through kirtan, I have been cooking meals for people for a while, and now I am teaching them how to cook or how to internalize the mantras for themselves."

What is mantra?

"The word mantra has a few different meanings," David begins. "Its actual root comes from the word 'mind.' When you put the two syllables together that form 'mantra,' it means to guide or protect the mind; in essence, into a more spacious, positive, connected, and loving state of being." David continues, "We all know the mind wanders, and it can get imposed upon by negativity and fear, so mantra helps shift one to a more holistic, connected, trusting, loving state of being."

I recently read about the mystic Florence Scovel Shinn, born in 1871 in Camden, NJ, who wrote *Your Word is Your Wand* and *The Game of Life*. In both texts, she talks about the most powerful two words being "I Am" and what we place after that. That how we speak, we create—that "death and life are in the power of the tongue." She references other source texts in her work. If you are interested in learning more, many of her books are now public domain and can be accessed online.

It is perplexing that we don't learn more of the power of our thoughts and words in school. Why are we taught anatomy but not neurology? I mean, we heard about sticks and stones, but it wasn't until I was in my mid-twenties, after my master's degree, that I began to hear about the power of persuasion and focused thought being bolstered by the vibration of how I talk to others, and most importantly to myself. Back to David's beautiful explanations:

"The mantras in the yogic traditions—there are mantras across many traditions—come from an ancient language that was revealed for the sole purpose of spiritual liberation, and that's called Sanskrit.

"The mantras that I work with," David continues, "work with the language of Sanskrit. Mantra is a sequence of syllables that are placed together to achieve certain kinds of results. You can say them quietly or out loud. In the practice I mentioned earlier, kirtan, you sing them. There is a musical element involved. There are many ways one can practice these mantras."

The melodic roots of a living language, in this case Sanskrit, can play across our mind and nervous system to a more positive effect. Sanskrit is not the only live, or vibrational, language. Many indigenous languages carry a vibration. We'll stay focused on Sanskrit here, but the properties of live languages upon neurology translate across cultures. The Vedic philosophies from which mantra and kirtan stem knew this about our human brain. These philosophies knew of our restlessness and our tendencies to need supportive practices to keep us aligned for our health and vitality.

"Mantra works on vibration, and we are made of vibration; we are made of energy, and the power of mantra is the vibration of the sound and its healing capacity," David says. "Most languages are symbolic in the sense that if I said the word 'apple,' the word is the symbol for the thing. There is a distance between the word and the thing that it is describing. [With] the word apple, you won't get the taste or the nourishment of the apple through the word, but in Sanskrit, especially in its mantra form, it's considered to be [a] non-symbolic language. So the sound of the word," David says as he snaps his fingers, "is exactly the same to which the word is pointing to. There's no mental or intellectual imposition that a practitioner has to bring to the mantra. The vibration of the sound does all the work."

I hold that one of the great benefits of practicing mantra is its ability to clear the slate. It is the same as cleaning the kitchen table. You have to wipe down the table, clear it of plates and dishes, and clean up the flower vase to make space for a peaceful and pleasurable meal. The same is true for our mind. If we do not pause to clear and clean the debris of the day, we are crowded and overrun, unable to relax and enjoy the nourishment of the present moment.

"Consider how much noise is out there in the world on so many levels," David offers. "I consider the mantra practice to be a real haven for the psyche... and extremely healing for the body, too. Whatever aspect of mind that has been drilling or driving at a person, when that's released, when that separative focal point dissolves, an opening takes place where healing happens. Now there are many ways that can happen, but mantra is a very powerful and ancient one. Because of its nature, the potency of the sound itself, it doesn't really require anything of us but to be in relationship to the sound."

All beliefs can be enveloped and held within this practice.

"Mantras are universal," David explains. "They work on the energy body of a human system. People of all religions and faiths can engage mantras in a variety of different functional ways that have nothing to do with belief, and I have always appreciated that about the yogic wisdom. You don't start with belief. You start with a hypothesis of your own spiritual journey, and you explore to see what shows itself for you as true for *you* in the unique way that each one of us has a dialogue with something greater than ourselves."

We can move forward with the mantras from an energetic or an archetypal format. Archetypes can be overlooked in the modern day, yet they are tools reminding us that our problems and the ways we alchemize them are at once distinct and also universal. Story and myth have served us for eons, just as these stories of Rebirth are being shared with you now. These are powerful tools that can avail us to our own path: *Oh, yes, this confusion is normal, I can cultivate the frequency of patience or courage.*

To be comfortable and curious within is to find, return, and expand your center as it changes. This practice is both a discipline and dissolution, a both/ and, if you will. We can see it when David opens and then releases his yoga studio. He was ready to walk his path differently, so his alignment served in his walking away confidently, as was the case when Stephanie Cohen left Kremer. The right answer is expanding and contracting, as are you. We don't come into this world alone, yet we birth ourselves. We are a deeply interconnected species—through energy, through belief, through laughter, love, and even deceit. Interconnection is more easily apparent the more we understand and attune to our own clarity, the more we stop leaning out of ourselves or away from ourselves.

David first used mantra when he was a teenager, inspired by his parents who had found Transcendental Meditation in the 1970s. At that time, he had one mantra and was sitting 20 minutes in the morning and 20 minutes at night for a structured practice. Although David supports a structured routine (or whatever serves *your* personal practice), he shares:

> "The beauty for me is being reminded to stay connected to your source. Ultimately where I come with that, is that everything serves as a reminder if you are paying attention.

> "I want to fortify people with the opportunity to be in relationship with these mantras. Sometimes people will think they don't have time for this. But honestly, the discipline of carving out a few minutes in your day to reconnect to yourself can end up saving you time because of the practice, the self-care of connection."

"Something that can bring us to center no matter where we are is precious," I affirm. David often teaches that mantra practice can coincide with taking a walk or making a cup of tea. Anything can serve as a reminder if you are paying attention.

Anything can serve as a reminder if you are paying attention.

It's important to note that we all take turns forgetting who we truly are, what we are capable of, and that we are connected to something larger. It's a part of our growth process. I believe the more we share our stories and our tools, the easier it becomes to remember who we are, what we are capable of, and why we are here.

"For me, mantra is the closest sound to silence," says David.

This sentence organically brought me backwards in time to when David and company were performing kirtans on Friday nights at Yoga on Main. I didn't exactly understand what kirtan was. I went with my friends from yoga teacher training, and I stayed because of the feeling of euphoria. I was in my twenties, and until kirtan, Friday nights more likely meant a party scene. Here, at kirtan, I had no fear of who was there or posturing of how I needed to act or sing. I was free. Those small nights of music gave me an early peek into another way of gathering and feeling into community.

"That's the beauty of all forms of yoga practice," David says, "that non-judgment. There is so much power in a person's voice and what is communicated. Everyone has a unique voice. So when there is a coming together of those diverse textures and diverse timbres in sound, that to me reflects a person's soul. It's a magical thing that takes place.

"It's a bunch of individuals singing, of course... in a very safe and connected space," David continues. "It goes from *I'm singing* and *you're singing* to *we're singing*, which is a more pleasant experience. But then kirtan goes one step deeper. It's not even *we're singing*—there are 50 people, but there is just one voice. It's like we have gone deeper to the source of the voice itself, and that's what—as a musician, that is why all of us play music, because suddenly we're up there with other musicians, and we're putting this finger there, and we're singing this note or that note, and we are doing so in harmony and unison with the rest of the band, and suddenly there is this moment where nobody is doing anything and music is just happening... Kirtan, which was calibrated for the sole purpose of spiritual alignment when you have everybody tuning into that simultaneously, it is very transformational."

I never thought, when I started going to kirtan, that I was making space or that I was attuning myself to an ancient language of archetypal energy. I loved it because I laughed, and I felt better when I left from the dancing and the euphoria of community. I was completely in the moment, and that's what spaciousness provides. As for the silence David mentioned—it's true. All that movement, the chanting and the vibration of joy, there would be this huge, silent pause between songs, and it was a long, cool drink of the sacred. It was silence full of connection. It was a respite. The movement created the stillness, like most yoga practices do. Like moving your body does on a good walk, or laughing until you cry with a good friend. Our present culture tells us to move faster, do more, do better, but I often find the clarity comes in the unsuspecting pauses, in the cracks between what we are so certain we know, and—whammo!—something else comes wafting through. A new direction, an answered prayer is revealed.

When we make space, miracles find their way, just like the patient wag of a dog's hopeful tail, a dog who, over a decade later, snores by my side, both us more seasoned and more intertwined than I could have ever known, holding stories between us that pulse through the ethers. How grateful I am that destiny took the reins, trusting that I would eventually open to the divine placement and learn to trust more.

"All is well consciousness," is what David coins the arrival of mindset with kirtan or mantra. You come to his mantra class feeling the weight of your life, and somewhere along the line, it drops—and "it's all is well consciousness. There is no real problem that you have to stress out about, you just feel the presence of something greater.

"In that moment, you feel: *Oh, well all the rest of the time, the greater presence isn't there. Until this moment, and it only shows up because we are engaged in this wonderful practice together.* But the truth is," David says honestly, "the practice enabled you to feel the presence. And the reality of that is the Presence—call it what you will: love, consciousness, connection—it's always there. *It's always there.* Just because you aren't aware of it doesn't mean it isn't there. That's where faith comes in. Like, if you are really struggling in a moment, just remember that although you may not be feeling connected or aware of the presence of this Grace, know it's still there. You're just somewhere else."

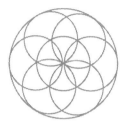

Beauty and Belief

Nothing is more demanding of space and trust than birth. If you look at it astrologically, you choose your star appointed moment with great precision. If you look at it ancestrally, you are the culmination of multiple lives making multiple (seemingly inconsequential) choices to enable the divine orchestrated event of you. Birth is a tremendous confluence of divinity and humanity. Birth is relevant. It matters not if you have had children—you are here. You have been birthed. Birth is a dance of grace and grit, announcing your arrival. How glorious.

After attending my first birth (not my own), I became convinced everyone would benefit from seeing a birth. Witnessing a baby's arrival helped me open more to life's majesty. The first birth I attended was on a coconut farm with a loving family and midwife at the helm. Although we were eventually trans-ported to the hospital, the mother ultimately gave birth of her own accord. As the moment of arrival drew near, I moved away from the mama's earth-grounding grip to the foot of the hospital bed to make space for the imminent arrival of the little one.

The tenor of the air in the room changes with birth. I shuffled away from the mama and unconsciously landed myself a front row seat, standing behind the doctor's shoulder, watching the crowning of this miraculous baby boy. I saw the fullness and retraction, and I saw what I would describe as a split moment of collapse as the final spiraling push of life happens, and baby emerges while mama succeeds in her sojourn.

It took me days to process what I saw and felt in that room. I had no idea then I would become a mother myself. I did know that I became fascinated with birth and the fact that, as humans, we know very little about our two assured journeys: birth and death.

> Birth is happening all around us.
> So is death.
> Death of people, ideals, opportunities, phases, and flowers.
> To deny one is to deny the other.
> To lean into one is to lean into the other.

It is the polarity of being here and human. It's the genesis of the spiral of our lives. It's also the pulse release of letting one attachment go to make space for a new dream. You really cannot have a rebirth without first having some sort of death. Many mothers will speak of the thinness of space between life and death at birth.

I had heard this and witnessed it, but I was unprepared for the death of expectation that would herald in both the birth of my son and the birth of me as a mama. From years as a holistic practitioner, I had a general belief that birth would happen; however, I also knew I had no idea what happened specifically after birth and what postpartum truly meant. When Terri Simmons, my midwife, explained that she stays with a post-partum woman until "her essence returns," I knew she was my chosen guide. Here was a woman who understood and honored the human body and her process. I had no idea the depth of that invitation until I walked the threshold myself.

Meet Terri Simmons

I am so elated to introduce you to Terri Simmons, community midwife, herbalist, teacher, and bodyworker specializing in trauma release. Terri is a

Certified Professional Midwife who has worked in Texas, Guatemala, Peru, Mexico, New Mexico, and Pennsylvania, in both clinical and non-clinical settings. She is now focused on educating and empowering midwives. Terri believes in the natural process and is in awe of the power of birth.

Birthwork for Terri started from a political place.

> "Independence has always been important to me; I wanted something I could travel around the world with and work with people. I wanted to work with women, something that had a natural component that I wouldn't get bored with, and have [the] self-agency that being a community midwife allows for. There really is a surgence of women and people taking charge of their lives, and that leadership comes from within as well as from without. Our community makes us. We have kinda lost that. There are opportunities to bring that back right now. I hope birth follows that. It is a scary place for a lot of people, and it doesn't have to be. But it is."

"It's a very human response to fear birth," I say. People either want to dive right in or push it away, consciously or unconsciously.

> "You cannot push away birth," Terri says, "you have to go through it. The only thing 'pushing away' does in birth is deciding not to be a part of it and staying on the outside of it. That's impossible at home unless your body just takes over. I've seen many births where the [mother] is along for the ride."

> Terri continues, "You cannot push it. You cannot pull it. You have to walk beside it. As the attendee of birth, it is the same thing. I cannot push it or pull it. I have to walk beside [it]. Sometimes that takes a lot of retraining the mind to what the possibilities are."

It turns out the possibilities are endless when it comes to birth, and I want to direct our consideration of those possibilities towards postpartum. You *have* the baby, which is often when the public stops feeling collectively connected, and yet it is exactly when the mother and new babe need the most grounding. The phase of the baby's arrival also means the mother's recuperation, and both need support and community.

So what *is* postpartum?

From the common definition: It is the time post-birth or post-pregnancy, whether that is a termination, miscarriage, or a birth. Terri teaches that each has an after-birth period.

As a culture, we are very excited for the pregnancy, and we have learned to drop off food for the baby's arrival. But what else is there? Terri explains that there is a remembering growing today of the impact the little one has, especially upon a mother, who is understandably tired and whose hormones are regulating.

> Terri shares, "People ask me all the time, 'Do you ask people to stay in bed for two weeks?' And I say, 'No, I ask them to hang out for 40 days.'" She laughs. "Every day that you are up, tack on another day of rest. And you can heal from birth at any time— there is no missed opportunity."

Integration of birth is always available. This is one of the most fascinating and exciting things that I have witnessed with Terri's work, my own post-birth experiences, and now with my clients. As Terri says, three, sixteen, or thirty-three years after your postpartum, the healing can begin.

What needs to be healed? Terri teaches that whatever is happening to you is normal because you are normal, and the next step is to understand what range you are in. Can you handle your experience, or do you need help? If you do not have a community or a point of reflection, sometimes understanding or voicing when a mother needs help can be confusing, even embarrassing, if natural cycles are not understood.

Terri clarifies, "[In pregnancy], baby is going to grow whether you eat this or that, sleep a lot or don't, exercise or don't—it's just going to grow. It's an amazing example that nature works. We need to nourish, and we'll be healthier. We eat better, the baby will be better. The fetus just takes from us, so it is kinda nice because then you can just look at yourself. If you are feeding yourself, then the baby is getting enough. Basically everything you feel physically, your baby is just one step behind you. This is the same postpartum."

"I want *everyone* to hear that," I squeal. "It is the same postpartum. Can you give us a window? Everyone talks about six weeks as a magical number, and I don't think that captures it."

"Well it depends on how your pregnancy was, how your pre-pregnancy was, what your support system is, then it can take longer," she explains. "Really we talk about it being the fourth trimester, and a trimester is three months. So I tell people not to gauge how they are supposed to feel until six weeks, and that gives the luxury of—*okay*. A bit of an exhale of relief, so to speak."

Terri continues, "It is kinda a magic number, six weeks. If things are falling into place well, you have good rest and good food, you have good fluids, and things are moving, then yes, [after] six weeks your hormones are probably going to reset. If you had a really hard first couple of weeks because of the breast feeding, recovering from possible trauma in the birth, or just you didn't expect things to go the way they did, even if it was a 'successful home birth,' it still can be shocking to the system. So you want to give yourself a break on comparing [your situation] to others.

"Because a lot of people will be like: *Oh it doesn't matter, you had a healthy baby.* No," she counters. "If you are upset, you're upset, and it's okay to be very grateful, and to be really pissed off. It really is okay to have parallel emotions. In fact, it is incredibly important to have parallels that you can identify. If you're loving it all the time, then you are good. If you are not loving it all the time, then you need to figure out where you can fill in those gaps to create that balance.

"We used to have the balance of the community. I'm sure there have always been times where that community has been off balance—but when we look at an ideal situation, it doesn't always have all the luxuries of the modern world," she shares. "It has somebody who you can enjoy holding your baby, so you have lots of rest. You don't have to ask for food or fluids—they're just brought to you. It's just assumed that you need to eat, and in fact most people when they are well taken care of have excess around them. It can be really simple. In fact, you are going through so much that your digestive system is already sorta compromised by a growing baby, and all your intestines being pushed out and your stomach being pushed up. Sometimes with misalignments, your intestines can [get] caught underneath your ribs—that can cause a lot of discomfort. Having a good posture during your pregnancy seems to be very key to having a really good birth."

Terri explains that many women have held a posture of keeping everything tucked in and tight versus letting it flow. The loosening of the pelvic area can be uncomfortable with this process, but Terri explains it is also a time to start letting your flexibility grow and becoming comfortable with pressure and being uncomfortable.

"You don't want to go against the pressure," Terri teaches. "That is where the baby's messaging is to come out, so if you are sensitive to the pressure, which a lot of people seem to have, you need to kinda wrap yourself around the idea that we are looking for *extreme pressure at the end.* That's the only way the baby is coming vaginally. Remembering that this is happening with—and not to—your body helps, too."

If you are sitting with a pregnancy currently or you see one on the horizon, there is a lot of dynamic wisdom that Terri shares. You may think, *Yeah, okay, pressure*. But somehow we have forgotten the intact system set up to signal birth and release. So yes, as awkwardly as we have been conditioned to not talk about it, at some point, you will feel someone's hands looking for an exit that is the internal curvature of your pelvis. It is weird. It is amazing, and it happens. It's birth.

> "Yeah, so that pressure includes pressure on your bladder. A lot of people tell me, *I cannot drink a lot because then I will just pee a lot*. Okay, then that means you are not absorbing. You shouldn't pee out what you drink in. You want to look to flax or chia seeds and put them in the bottom of your water to help bring in good electrolytes. Get some good mineral salts (sea salts if you know its origin, not refined salt) and put that in your water, or add lemon—all to keep everything pliable and absorbing well, maybe pre-, during, or post-pregnancy. I know we are focusing on post, but it often starts before that."

Simple choices add up, and confusion often occurs in moments of great change and transition. Common sense can often be a smidge out of reach if we are unhinged in an expansive or transitory phase. In the midst of raising her three children, I had a good friend say, "I am noticing most of my problems can be solved by staying hydrated." I chuckled at her truth. What you drink has a ripple effect on how you feel. It can be that profound from a body level.

There are two points of awareness to highlight here: One, big problems can often be adjusted by simple measures. And two, your health stasis affects everything. So if you are out of whack in hydration, it can show up in frustration, or as Terri explains, even in a pregnant woman's posture. It can make you harried while writing a work proposal or doubtful of a new creative project. When we are flowing and nourished, it is easier to weather the currents of every day.

"Dehydration will affect your posture because if you have less fluids, you are going to have more pain, and you tend to go away from the pain in your body, which often develops bad posture. Right? For example, if everyone just sits up right now," Terri teaches, "you are going to find the sensitive spots in where a good posture mode is. When you are in good posture mode, your ribs are not flared in. There is no space in between. And [it] is very important to keep that posture. As I was saying before, your intestines are going to be pushed out of the way as your baby grows in your uterus, so the stomach is going to move, the gall-bladder gets moved; everything is getting pushed away."

Right.

Exhale, feet on the floor, or at least into a comfortable moment, and watch three releasing breaths move through your body. Let's go get a glass of water before we keep going and drink in a little appreciation for this body self.

Reminders of our body's inner workings and connectivity to our mindset can help us find our way back to center. If I am panicked or faithless about the future, so too does my physical body falter from this perspective. Of course, we know this. We *know* this. We can tell when someone is walking towards us if they are doing so with confidence or hesitance. We can even see the workings of a bad day hanging on a good friend. The great news is every time we turn towards alignment, alignment turns towards us.

"Whenever you feel unsafe with something you sit with it, you put your hand on your heart and sit with that unsafe feeling and try to identify where that is coming from. If you can place it, you can often help heal it.

"Without even placing why—you just push it away," Terri clarifies. "I have been saying for years and years: A clear mind is a clear birth. But how the heck do you get there? More recently, I have been saying we need this clear space for this baby to come through. Sometimes you just have to push all that crap that you got in your brain out of the way. It's almost like, it's okay to clear a path. It doesn't mean your stuff is gone, you are just clearing a path and saying this is not the time to deal with that. Now stuff that keeps popping in your path as you are trying to clear it—that is stuff worth exploring. As you're having that metaphor of good posture, when you have good posture, you actually have more self-esteem. You actually have more self-regulation. You have that self-efficacy." Terri's voice smiles.

"What is self-efficacy, Terri?" I ask.

"If you can believe it, then you can achieve it," she answers.

I know that Terri wondered if this statement was too over simplified or egoic. It isn't when contextualized or allowed to be witnessed for its naked truth. For me, to understand this invitation to power and self-sovereignty, you must begin to move from a space where your internal power can rise and reside. The cornerstone of that power is your belief. It is funny to me when people call manifestation "new age" because it is not. If you look in ancient scriptural texts across cultures, the origin of the mind is the manifestation of the world.

If you can believe it, then you can achieve it.

Once you allow the concept of deciding and finding what you need to magnetize into your life, you can take the invitation primarily in two ways. You can move from manifesting parking spots—like the nineties movie *The Secret* used as a teaching tool—to jobs and relationships, et cetera. Or you can use that idea of deciding and begin to seek inside without judgment. What beliefs have I decided are true? What neural mappings have I reinforced about the way my life, my wealth, my birth, my body has to be? Why do things seem to happen this way? What the bleep is going on in my subconscious? Because maybe I don't want to magnetize that anymore. Maybe I want to make space for another perspective. Maybe I want to shift from ardent knowing to expansive curiosity. Maybe, as Terri invites us, we want to clear some space. Feel into *where* the things we are birthing are coming from and decide if that is what we want to build upon.

Sounds overly simple? Well sure, the truth always does.

> *Have faith*
> *Follow your own shining*
> *Be aware of your own awareness*
> *On the darkest nights you will not stumble*
> *On the brightest days you will not blink*
> *This is called*
>   *"The Practice of Eternal Light"*
>
> — Verse 52, translated by Jonathan Star from the
>   *Tao Te Ching* by Lao Tzu

The simplicity *is* your journey. You cannot hide from your journey; you cannot push it or pull it, you have to walk it, as Terri says.

> "Self-efficacy comes from having had successful situations in your life. It can come from seeing other people have that success or being encouraged that you can do it. There have been so many times that I have been holding space for somebody to just believe that they can do this, especially when they get into a situation they didn't expect—and that is where resilience comes in. You can trust the process so much that you can trust even the unexpected—because we can learn from all of it. It's not a place to judge."

Belief is the single strongest medicine we can give ourselves. Belief is what sold Mompops' miniature popsicles from farmer's markets to becoming a national brand that still cares about each child. Belief is what made Lisa O'Rear decide that even though life had taken a drastic turn, there was a guided reason for her to thrive again. Belief that the answer would come helped Christina walk away from an entrenched marriage and business to a new, loving life. Belief is what gives us the courage to greet each day with hope. Belief that there is another way is why you are holding this book in your hands.

> "When we take this back to postpartum, believing no matter what has happened, when we look around, we see that there are a lot of babies on the planet—so this must be normal." Terri then drops the truth of all truths: "I think that a big part of the postpartum healing is that you will never be the same, and that is okay."

"That is a *really* big point," I affirm. Perhaps because I am slender of build, the message I often received during postpartum was, *Oh, you're back*. And I was perplexed. What did that mean? What was "back"? I wasn't on a trip. I have a human now, and a scar to prove it. Going through any large transition, either of growth or loss, changes you, which is why space for integration, for the exhale and the stillness, is so important. You can push reality away, but that doesn't change that *you* need the time and space to understand and recreate your world. For some, this is easy and joyous, for others, maybe not—for all, there is learning.

> "There is a reason why for many generation[s] and millennia, women took time to heal after birth," Terri reminds us. "It's gonna take a lot of time, rest, fluids, and support to recover well. We have these myths now that two weeks is enough."

When Terri hears new moms say, "If I don't get out now, I am never going to get out," she knows it's the brain talking, not the body.

"It's the cry for normalcy. Something understood from before or getting back to a place that doesn't exist, rather than settling into the new normal. If you are fighting against the body and follow the pleas of the brain, you'll find yourself exhausted, then you'll start bleeding more, and then you are wondering why," Terri teaches. "You're at week three, and you're not better, and everyone else is better. There are some people that really do recover very quickly. It really depends on individuality and accepting that individuality."

I asked her to talk a smidge about the brain's development because moms often talk about a fog, and I didn't know it was biological and not just exhaustion.

"Not only are your hormones shifting to a new pattern—hopefully a good set of patterns—your brain is redistributing its grey matter. We have this incredible capacity to grow our brain, and one of the really incredible places is post birth," she affirms.

Terri told me the postpartum brain continues to redistribute for two years, and I have heard mothers comment that during their child's second year, they felt more space inside their heads. I have also witnessed clients integrating their birth journeys years after the fact. So has Terri. She shares that 10, 16, 30 years after birth, there is still availability to heal and integrate. Terri suggests that this relates to all birthing or threshold moments. If for whatever reason in the moment of your life, because of age or circumstance, you were unable to digest and integrate, what a joy to realize it is never, ever too late to find a new equilibrium, to locate a center, at once emboldened and softened by life's wisdom.

"So how can you address postpartum when your child is 10 years old?" I ask Terri.

"The first thing is stopping and accepting that you didn't take the time."

This can be a layered step in a healing journey.

"So here and now, we stop and take the time to acknowledge we didn't take the time before," Terri says compassionately. "Stop and write a few things down." She suggests an example: "If I could have had the most ideal situation, what would it be?" She continues, "One of the exciting things right now, as we learn about the brain and repatterning: We can recreate, give space for new programming, new blueprints. So accepting that you have something to heal, that you have something to reprint is *really* important."

And true to form, Terri adds candidly, "That's free and private. It's okay to be like, *Wow, I was in a crummy situation.* Or, *I didn't even know that there was this.* That's okay. Now we have more knowing, more access to things like this. But we didn't in the past."

A perspective to gently remember as you excavate these terrains, too, whether alone or with a professional.

In terms of birth specifically, it was the look in women's eyes when I talked about my postpartum care that prompted me to share Terri's wisdom on Rebirth. Listen, I honestly had my mind set (maybe too set, maybe too much of a doer and not enough surrender) on a home birth. I was 41 years old. I know a woman's body can do it. I thought my body could do it, but alas we had to have a hospital C-section after 36 hours of labor.

The hospital thought I was crazy. Did you know that a 41-year-old pregnant woman is called geriatric? I had two great-grandmothers that had "geriatric" pregnancies. We used to call them the surprise children. Anyway, I was completely defeated by going to a hospital. I am not calling the hospital a defeat. Rather, I am articulating how I felt at that moment. I remember when I laid on that hospital gurney, I felt utterly beaten. Here I was, a bodyworker that taught other women to empower themselves and their bodies, and my body had failed me. It doesn't matter if that is true. It took me a long time to sit and be honest with *how* I felt. Once I articulated the gnarly truth of how I felt, there was space for healing.

I remember the postpartum visit. Terri looked at me and said, "Let's go look at your scar."

I froze. Nope. I did not want to do that, my mind said as my legs followed her to the back bedroom. I had been doing the best job possible of avoiding my scar entirely.

I did not want to touch it. Accept it. Do anything with it.

"It's really big, I think," I shared.

"Not really. Looks about right."

"Oh. It's kinda red," I said.

"Nah, looks about right in texture and color. Healing nicely."

I couldn't feel that comment at all. Terri would later tell me this was a common reaction for many women: not wanting to touch the scar.

She explained why we wouldn't want adhesions.

"What?" I climbed into the moment.

"Well," she gingerly explained, "it's not just the skin that was cut, so was muscle, and so was your uterus."

My mind hit an iceberg of comprehension. This was not just an incision. This was layers. Layers of body and layers of feelings. A subtlety that could be missed or dodged. For me, this was a profound invitation. Without being rushed out of the moment, I thought about the expanse each layer of tissue had grown, the depth of fortitude the uterus had girded to safeguard this child, and those intricacies of flesh and depths of spirit needed me to sit still to heal. And they needed to be held, not shunned or shamed.

So we massaged the scar tissue until slowly, unweighted by trauma, a new alignment formed, a new assertion of strength emerged. It would take more than one moment; it would take months of revisiting this practice and feeling the once-frozen feelings melt and release with awareness. But what I got in return for sitting with that discomfort was integration for my body and my mind. I didn't have to wait for those frozen feelings to manifest and demand my attention. For this, I am forever grateful to Terri and committed to passing this wisdom on.

In the midst of my postpartum journey, even in the beginning, when I would say: "I had a midwife," many people would respond: "Oh, I thought you gave birth in the hospital."

"I did."

"And you had her, too?"

"Yes."

"What did she do?"

"Come and check on me and my son. See that I was coming back into balance, answer questions, help navigate breastfeeding—those kinds of things," I would answer, although there was indeed more, especially in the realm of re-establishing mind-body-spirit connection.

"Wow. How long?"

"About eight weeks."

And that is when I would see a flash of shock. In some cases tears. That reaction is what rooted my commitment to sharing my story, these stories, and the possible reclamations of birth. What I saw in their eyes was the shock that this help exists, *for everyone*.

There is so much that can be done with postpartum work that is beyond cleaning the house and watching kids (although that is deeply needed). It is recognizing what we so often rush past: making time to be in the present moment and digest. Terri mentions that many current conversations about postpartum focus on the external or the gadgets—the externals and not the internals. The slowing down to allow the body to realign. She reminds us that we need to slow down and look back. The way we look at birth is exceptionally modern, and we are forgetting that a few generations back, we were birthing at home; we were moving through this phase differently. It's a choice. All birth has a multitude of choices, including postpartum. I would say that to be true of any birth. As a society, as a community, we have to want that integration and make space for it.

Terri invites us to consider birth and postpartum as non-medical, no matter how it occurs, and how that can create room and really soften us to the experience. She expounds,

> "Many of us don't interface regularly with the medical world other than knowing someone that may work in it. So when a woman becomes pregnant and goes to the hospital, there is an idea that can arise that 'I don't know how to do this.' But we do know—we have been living in these bodies. We are the authority of our bodies. We might need to reflect out to see where we need to reflect back in to help manage a situation. For sure, sometimes we need help, so we ask for it; we need to accept that help."

Back to that moment we think that we have lost. The body holds the story. Terri tells us to create and allow that "clear space." The door doesn't close on you to reclaim that space or integration—as a mother, as a business owner, a divorcee, the list goes on. The door to healing does not close. This reclamation does not mean that you get to rewrite history, it means that the scar no longer stops growth. Whatever gets stretched or moved for birth, literally or metaphorically, there is an emotion attached to that expansion. When that emotion is integrated, we come back to center, stronger.

> "If you want to get rid of something, you have to accept picking it up and getting rid of it. You can't will it away," Terri shares. "If you look around your house, there are things that you don't want. But you cannot will them away. Same with the things in our body. You have to pick them up, acknowledge them to

remove them—you cannot will them away. Like the scar tissue. We have to work on it. We have to figure out, what is the individual way or release?"

When people reach out to Terri, especially in mid-birth, and say they can't do it anymore, her first response is to "not fall for that," which makes me chuckle. As humans feel the magnitude of a life bursting—whether with a child, business, book, or change—just at that precipice, we may feel the overwhelming desire to run away. That we cannot go on. Yet we do. At that juncture, the birth is happening.

"You may not know what you need in your medicine bag, or who you need, or what you will need from whom, including yourself, but it is going to happen. Plenty other people have jumped off that cliff—and you can too," she cheerleads practically.

"If you go with the flow instead of fighting it, it is going to go a lot more healthy in the long run. If you don't have what you wanted, you have your fallbacks on resilience. You can only look for the positive in the negative, and the negative in the positive. Your choice to look for possibilities in the positivity. It's the healthy balance."

Terri is careful to reiterate that there has to be a healthy balance, and birth is ultimately unpredictable. We have to stay focused on the goals and be available to the unexpected. You never know.

"Listen," she says, "if you drop that cup, we can pick it up. We might not be able to repair it, but we can transform it into something else. It can become something else. That's the beauty of it. What you go through makes you beautiful."

What possibilities become available when we know the door to healing does not close? When we honor that the body does indeed hold the story, yet is equally willing to let it go, miraculous spaciousness can appear.

Is there room today to reawaken to the brilliance of birth, your own or one happening right now as we read, sending out its own ripple upon our one human family and existence? In a modern world, how do we open to the innate simplicity of being with what is, demanding both our courage and our surrender, calling us to be humble and proud at the very same time? Can we let all these elements fan the fires of belief in ourselves and our ability to rise?

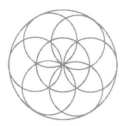

Doubt and Grace

Elder and *Teacher* are words that don't fall as frequently these days as a human spirit needs them. For whatever reason, I was born to younger parents and had the gift of being quite close with both sets of my grandparents. I was held very deeply by them in big ways, like trips to Disney World and Germany, and little ways, like rings of strawberries in a sugar jar and singing songs together on car rides to dinner. I believe this inlay of *Elder* made an entrée into my psyche about the nuance of living and the tenor that elders hold. Although both sets of grandparents were very grounded in their living in Philadelphia, PA, they both served in feeding my curiosity and my appetite for travel. Travel has led me to meet and learn what I didn't know that I didn't know. There is so much wisdom and difference and gloriousness out there for us, that as my dear friend, Elder, and Kumu Uncle Alva, taught, we need great humility to be able to see it.

And what is there to see? Everything. There is so much to see in one moment that we could be overwhelmed. That's why the slow wisdom of our grandparents' cadence or even the antiquity of knowledge can help us fast humans not miss the beauty that is all around us.

When I was fresh out of college and hot to trot at my new technical marketing job in silk suits and dangerous shoes, shaking my fist at every grievance, squealing my outrage over the kitchen table, my grandfather, the simple sage that he was, said to me: "Kid, you are either here (*he raised his hand*) or here (*he lowered his hand*)—you wanna be here..." His steady, patient hand moved across the midline. And he never did tree pose or attended a Vipassana retreat. He simply came from a time that appreciated the moment. I'm still striving to live that straight and steady line.

I love yoga and meditation, and they are definitely tools in my toolbox with today's fast pace, yet if I am only slow on my mat, and I cannot slow down for myself or to show kindness to others... the practice means nothing.

That is simple Elder wisdom.

Meet Lilavati

I met Lilavati over a jar of jasmine eye cream. It is as luxurious as it sounds. At the time, my eyes were so dry from the city soot that I was having trouble with my contacts. Standing in her Philadelphia brownstone known as the Bharani Temple, adorned in velvet and pictures of deities, I knew that this was not the average beauty product.

Lilavati is an Ayurvedic practitioner that explains herself to be a "potions master, devoted servant to beauty's alchemy, creating sacred scent plant-based ritual tools for sublime beauty and health." One of the most precious gifts she offers is the silence to connect to one's own self. It is neither her age-defying wild mane, her contagious laugh, nor her honest compassion that holds my attention. It is her brutal honesty and her get up again-ness that makes her a most treasured gem. Lilavati's voice tells you so much about her. Her lilt carries you off into a world of your own, leaving you restored and nourished without the effort of the mind, but rather with the clear guidance of the body.

The eye cream's efficacy intrigued me, and I began attending her yoga classes, which were also draped in deep reds and purples. Contrary to the exertion and competition that was rolling through many yoga studios, I found myself very rarely standing in her class but dropping deeply into the ley lines of beingness and finding deep release and reset. I knew that yoga and spiritual sciences were here, and I also knew lineal practitioners were fewer and farther between these days.

There is a grand movement inviting us to rest more these days, and I can get behind that. I also think there is a place to look at the sthira and sukha, Sanskrit terms for the simultaneous efforts of striving and resting. The effort and the grace. When we endeavor to create, we may strive many times over for a finished product. Or we may be creating, creating, creating, and years later we hit a stride unimaginable. Let's pan the camera out—not versus anything, but encompassing everything—and melt a little into the spiral of being.

"You have been doing this from early on," I say to Lilavati as the sunlight dances across the temple floor.

> "Yes, from very young. So I got a lot of insight into nuance. I don't know what it is about the human that I am, I have this capacity to feel other humans' pain and other humans' plights and tensions..."

At around 16 years of age, there was a confluence of events in Lilavati's path. In the early seventies, a revolution of natural therapy was booming, and a health food store opened down the street from where she lived in Yardley, PA. At the same time, many members in her father's large Italian family were getting cancer. She began educating herself on holistic practices and analyzing her family's lifestyle.

> "My father was a butcher, and here I was, 16 and declaring myself a vegetarian and telling my family everyone is getting catnip enemas!" Lilavati declares. "I was passionate because I was seeing my family's horrific demise, and I was saying, 'Look, you are creating this by what you are taking into your body, and there is a way to alleviate some of these symptoms.'"

While this passion awakened, she attempted film school, and when that evaporated, she came back home and decided to become a makeup artist or massage therapist. She moved to New York, becoming enchanted with British fashion magazines and the culture they illuminated, and off she went to Europe to become an aesthetician, studying herbology, massage, and aromatherapy, too. To position herself lucratively, she came back to the United States to work in the salons and study "everything that had to do with healing the body. That was my twenties."

At the end of her twenties, she married and had a child, leaving the salon environment and eventually working with clients from home. In the beginning of the nineties, which was her mid-thirties, again a cross-section of journeys occurred with a Bikram Hot Yoga opening down the street from her.

> "Then all of the sudden, I'm like, *this is what I want*. I find Kripalu. In the nineties, you had to make pilgrimages. That's what I did, I made pilgrimages to teachers. I was determined to find the best teacher in the world that was the most honored, and that is the teacher I am going to study with. And I did that over, and over, and over again."

"What in you—how did you know—you were in a good space with a teacher?" I ask Lilavati to clarify.

> "Most of the teachers, they were alright. When I found my tantra teacher, my spiritual teacher, that was a done deal. I happened to be in Philly one day and saw this poster on the wall, and it said: 'Chakras Therapy in New Hope, PA,' and I was like, *Yeah, right!* Because I grew up near there. I end up going to this gathering of beings, and there is this beautiful Indian woman who walks out and starts talking about Shiva and Shakti making love at the crown chakra and tears just start pouring down my eyes. *Here's my teacher.* All the other teachers, I thought, *Yeah, they know stuff*, but this one was like—" and Lilavati makes the sound of an explosion, a mind blown, a resonance found. "This is everything."

When you journey towards something and keep going, you can feel the rightness of it, and your life will make sure you know it. It does not matter if you believe in lifetimes of knowledge or want to learn about Shiva and Shakti. What does translate across lives and dharmas is this: If you commit to the passion that was instilled in you upon your birth, your path will lead you to the places that seek you, the places that wait for you. One of my favorite Hafiz quotes whispers:

Wherever you have
Dreamed of going,
I have camped there,
And left firewood
For when you arrive.

We cannot know unless we embark upon the journey, until we trust the not knowing. When we settle into the striving and trusting is when unexpected grace arises. I know this, and *still* I have to walk myself away from my habits of pushing and pushing. The more I spiral around the years of my life, the more I feel like I am being beckoned to surrender and trust. Different phases of life call for different phases of learning.

Lilavati explains, "I think that's when you're ready to learn is when you realize that there is an endless stream of knowledge that we will never really touch fully and completely, but if we are able to press up against it for a moment or two—"

"It's complete grace," I let slip out.

"It's complete grace," she affirms.

"It's much easier to say *I know that* then to humble yourself no matter where you are," I continue.

"Exactly," she says. "As soon as you say *I know that*, you learn nothing—in everything."

"Could you speak to us a little about tantra?" I ask, since there is a lot of confusion about what this lineage is.

"Tantra at its base, from my vantage point, is a way to connect deeply with this moment in time through the wisdom of the elements. It's based on practices: mantra, mudra, breathwork, movement—but it's also based on a connection to fields of consciousness that we call deities, which means energy. Energy is everything. It's a weaving of experiencing life in this moment of time without the bondage of the past interfering."

"Can you explain the technology or precision employed in your classes?"

"What is yoga has become distorted. [When you] try to enter the world of yoga through the physicality of being tense and tight, there is no opportunity to release the tensions that we have accumulated through our daily life to land into nothingness. To feel what is available that rises up to direct us into a state of wisdom and response. That might sound very confusing, but we have to land first."

Lilavati decodes an example for us: "Many people may think, *If I hold Warrior II for long enough, I will get what I want.* Which, if it's distilled down to its essence, it's: *I want to be loved. I want to be embraced. I want to be seen. I want to be heard. I want to be experienced for the human I am.* And we're all working really too hard for that."

"What I am hearing is we're doing the opposite," I offer. "We cannot run up to someone, grab them by the shoulders, and say, *Love me.*"

"Exactly, that's what our psyches and our bodies are doing," Lilavati clarifies. "Our bodies are saying, Wait a minute, I've been racing around all day listening to your fear-generated suggestions, and now you are pushing me even farther. A lot of times people will say after a yoga class that they feel so good, but they are in shavasana at the end, doing nothing. I'd have to say that tantra distills us down to the nothingness so we may be present and be."

"You mention people coming to class and being still and feeling into the pain that is in their knee. Why is that significant?" I ask.

> "Because the cosmos is within us," she answers. "Every aspect of consciousness is in this body. All beauty, all ease, all that we seek to attain in this consciousness is within ourselves at every given moment. We just have to untangle the knots that prevent us from feeling these experiences within ourselves. It's so applicable because we live in a hard and harsh time."

Dismantling is arduous.

Often in her classes, Lilavati mentions that our next day is not guaranteed; this truth tumbled over me in a forward fold. I realized, it's not so common anymore to talk about shavasana as corpse pose; the many yoga playlists have become louder and louder to drown out the truth within ourselves that we are limitless and mortal. I found myself settling into her quiet reminder that the more we consume, the more bloated and extended away from ourselves we are. The modern pace leaves little time for digestion.

The cosmos is within us.

So what are we to do? We *want* to create. We *want* to build. What is there for us to stay in balance? We cannot go back, but we can return to center with what we learn.

> "It is imperative for us to anchor into an inherent trust in our lives, a trust that we know is time tested, and we believe beyond anything else," Lilavati states. "It becomes crucial to go within to find rituals and methods to find our faith in our day-to-day process. We are so seduced by the outer. There is so much to draw our attention outward; it gets so confusing. Ultimately, it diminishes one's faith."

"I think a lot of people are confused, including me," I say. "Confusion seems innocuous, but it is actually diabolical and causes tremendous disruption."

> "Tremendous disruption because it permeates every aspect of life; it's like a stink—an aroma. It has a tendency to meander into every aspect of life," she confirms.

"And sometimes it is insidious because it gets into the small things, like, I don't know what to eat," I admit. "And I just stand there at the refrigerator, disabled."

> "Exactly," she agrees. "The way that we eat is such a rote activity. We grab foods we have eaten before. It is actually a real journey to eat well, and there is so much confusion around that, too. Because there is so much information that is available seducing us to do this or do that. *This is the miracle cure*, or *This is the path to enlightenment*," she mimics. "And there is so much more to it than: *Just pay me the money and you'll get there, too*."

We laugh.

We laugh because it is true and truly ridiculous.

> There is no five-step solution to live *your* life.
> There is help.
> There is insight.

There might even be sound advice, but you are the only one that can live your life, wading through doubt, clearing the space for grace.

Many self-help books, business books, and even spiritual science books will tell you to make a plan, create a habit, make a practice. It doesn't have to be glorious, yet it needs to be applicable to you. Let me give you an example: I have always loved the quiet of mornings. There have been years in my life where I went out of my way to stop at a favorite coffee shop before teaching. Then there were decades that I set my alarm for a 20-minute yoga practice, then there were mornings for an exercise practice. I then stumbled into an expansive decade where my mornings were languid and ruminative, and I could walk on the beach and come home and journal or pray before my day. Then I got plopped into the no-morningness of childrearing, and it was deeply destabilizing. I was missing the slowness that I had lost. I had turned on the spiral, and I needed to orient to what was, as well as what was available to me. I created my own ritual, and it went like this:

Before I turned on any lights, I lit a candle in the kitchen to set my intention for the day. I prepped my coffee, and as it brewed, I walked over to the front window to greet the morning sun and turn to pause in each of the directions: east, south, west, and north. I made it a small practice to orient myself in my life and on the earth before I busted into the business of shuttling into the demands of my day. For a few minutes, the morning was mine, and it made a big difference.

"I teach people [how to] engage in daily rituals, to anchor the mind and find trust and peace. I teach them daily rituals based on the energy of the Elements. How to go in everyday and have access, awareness, and gratitude toward Earth, Water, Fire, Space, and Air," she explains. "A simple example is the food that we eat. Have gratitude for where the food came from and how it came into our life. Or how our actions through the fire element create or destroy something... This can become a very long topic," she directs towards me, a warning that these are simple and profound concepts that can take an entire discipline to understand and are simultaneously available to everyone who acknowledges them. "I have been in the throes of these practices for so long I understand these elements and where they are in the body," Lilavati says humbly.

"I teach from the vantage point of, *What's right here? What element is right here?* And it is a day-to-day thing. I am directed by the Nakshatra (Vedic astrology), or the Planetary wisdom of the day imbued in the consciousness—but I never *plan* what I am teaching. It is always: land on the mat and download what is coming through, and let's work with that. This is how it becomes an organic experience. Because the Elements have power. Planets have vortexes. There is this big realm outside of ourselves that is manipulating our environment. Confusion comes a lot of times when we think we have to manipulate a lot—that we're the ones holding the stars in the sky. We have to do this and do that, and if we don't do this and that, this terrible thing is going to happen, and then I am going to feel guilt or regret or resentful—and therein lies the confusion. It takes a long time to just go in and negotiate around the B.S. of our own illusions, fears, and self-doubt."

Lilavati shares a story of witnessing a friend that was enmeshed in a problem in her life. She explains that when big problems arise, they can block out the rest of the world. She gave her friend this recommendation:

"Just imagine yourself. See yourself. Take yourself out of this enmeshment. Rise up and gaze upon your life as if you were telling the story of your life. You were 20 and this happened, or you were 36-six and this happened. And as a woman or man at 45, what happened? We have a tendency to put so much energy and tension in one scenario at a time that we lose track of the bigger picture and develop patterns of tension."

Tension, rather than remembering that we are as vast as the universe and that life is happening with us not to us. If you have read this book from cover to cover, an unexpected pattern has emerged. Inspired action is what arises from being present even if we don't know where it is leading us just yet. The title of this book happened before my conscious comprehension. I had to write it to understand it. I was led. The whole journey has been a form of leading, the smallness of each step being its own journey. Deciding to do the podcast. Reaching out to people I knew, making time for the project. Then reaching out to people I didn't know. Asking for help, believing in the service of the mission to inspire others and offer episodes as resources. I had to learn to use the podcast equipment. Not a big deal, but it could have been a deal-breaker. I had to learn that doing something out of pure joy needed to take up space even when there were other things I could have put my energy towards. I could go on. You'll learn in the next chapter how this book wound up in your hands.

The mission to help was wide. The how was unknown and continues to change. The way is what makes it all possible. The path, the maintenance of checking in with myself as to why I am here now, living, and what I need to ensure I thrive is a *constant* process. At times I can go really wide and see more than I can say, then in the next breath a wave of doubt and lack of worth can knock me off, if my stance is not strong. Fear is inevitable. Our focus is a choice. When I have a focus, a mission, a purpose, my strides keep going. It is when I lose that focus and allow myself to doubt that I become lost.

Enter structure, ritual, and life cycles. They help. They are designed to. Daily rituals help us open up our presence and make space in our day and in our bodies. Choosing to ingrain a road to the Divine, to what we believe in, to our greatness makes it much easier to be found when lost. When that enmeshment happens (because it will, as Lisa O'Rear reminded us), when the obstacle is bigger than life itself, we can come back to Lilavati's question: What is right here and right now?

It can open the aperture for unconsidered possibilities, like Terri Simmons mentioned, for grounding, for being as kind to yourself as possible. Whether the idea of planetary influence is new or something that is already a part of your daily knowing, we can all wiggle the toes of our own existence. When we soften our not knowing and let ourselves dip into the waters of our own wisdom, life can get a lot easier and sweeter. When we hold our vastness and the discipline of a commitment, we can work with the polarity rather than getting lost in it.

> "We can become more creative and even work with the Elemental nature when we have a structure to do so in a different way because it is not so vast. What I have pressed into as an intention for our last seasonal cleanse is: What is right in front of me? What is calling me right in this moment?" Lilavati explains, intimating that everything starts right here where we are.

You're here. Your body is here, too. It has all the stories digested and undigested in it, and it is waiting for your permission to let go and make that space for grace. Making space is a powerful practice.

Can I tell you something? I literally used to laugh at people who told me to put my hand on my heart and just *feel it*. *C'mon guys*, I would think. It doesn't get much more woo woo than that. Then you know what happened one day? I was living with a midwife. She had a stethoscope, and she asked if I had ever listened to my own heartbeat.

Nope. I hadn't.

She left it on the coffee table and told me I was welcome to give it a try.

Curious, I picked it up after she left the room. I laid on the couch, I set myself up, and when I heard the courageous beat of my own life, a tear involuntarily dropped down my face. I was in awe of her power. And I had never, not for one minute of my healthy three decades of life, given my heart one conscious thought until then.

I am still learning to open to the vastness of what the body knows. What the body holds. As a practice now, from time to time, in reverence or as a way to ground myself, I place my hand on my heart with presence and gratitude. Maybe one day you'll try it if you haven't already.

> "The oath behind Aromabliss is this," Lilavati explains of her Ayurvedic products and services, "if it does not enhance beauty (and that is a vast realm), health, and an experience of an elevated consciousness, it's got nothing to do with me. I cannot be part of it. Each one of these products is insinuating itself into all aspects of our consciousness. It is not just for ourselves that this exists. We care and create health for ourselves which will eventually turn into beauty. I am getting healthier so I can feel a level of consciousness, so I can see where my bullshit reigns supreme and where I can adjust through that. After that happens, beauty just exists. It exists in all facets of consciousness. It is not relegated to

the way something looks or our opinion of what it is. It is the diffusive beauty of this existence.

"We're born. We exist. And we're all gonna die. And the beings that we love so much—they are going to leave our sphere, and they will not be there for us in the way we think that they should be there for us, or do what we think they need to do. The whole essence of Aromabliss (Lilavati's Ayurvedic products) attends to generating autonomous bliss when everything falls apart."

"I don't always stop for Beauty," I admit to Lilavati. I think I had a habituated pattern to be happy with enough and not more than is necessary. It's the always grabbing for what will do, rather than commanding and expanding into a more luscious option. I rejected the commercialization of beauty long ago; however, reevaluating it as an act of expansion, both internally and externally, for my own life only happened for me through age and perspective shifting.

She quietly acknowledges, "What I have come to realize is that there is such a cosmos within ourselves that we are so bamboozled into believing that there is something that is going to get us off from the outside. And we are being forced to go inside and journey through this cosmos. And by applying these oils, which are ritualistic tools by which we can feel the embodiment of everything, not to be confused, but supported by it."

The most dynamic medicine brings us back to ourselves.

"The last few years have been very dynamic for me," Lilavati shares. "A lot of karmas have reached fruition. This is something that happens. It happens in a couple of places. It happens when someone is on a stringent spiritual path, and when one is not."

I chuckle at her vastness and candor.

"This lends itself to why these rituals are so damn important. In the last few years, my father left his body, and it was a very intense experience as that was happening. And at the same time, my child was—and still is—going through a very challenging time. My child is in her twenties and was really close to my father. My mother is having nervous breakdowns. I am really on the frontlines of a lot of experiences that have to do with life and death on a regular basis.

"When we are in the throes with family," she continues, "sometimes we are fused right in the center of it, and we are looking at it—even if we have information that can direct their lives in a different, more fruitful, more expansive, better (that we believe) way, it doesn't matter. It doesn't matter. Because they want their opinion. When we hold on to what we believe will assist the situation, it will cause great suffering, and then it lends itself back to deep self-introspection. It is imperative for us to get comfortable with what our line is. Where we draw the line in the sand. We can either fall apart defending what we believe is right or where we let go and take care of our own stuff.

"Even when we are called to the frontlines over and over and over again, the mirrors still lift up. I gotta work with this. My reactivity. There is this dynamic situation, but I still have to keep looking at my response mechanisms through these times of real intensity. I am not the only one that has heartbreak and headache and diabolical confusion with family members. We all do. Sometimes I wish I knew nothing about nothing," Lilavati ends honestly.

"Yes! Me too," I say with relief. "Because sometimes I feel ashamed that I will participate in behaviors that *I know better* than doing what I just did, dropping into patterns and frustrations that get me nowhere."

"We do. We get very exhausted dealing with emotional issues with the beings that we love. It is so exhausting. From what I have gleaned through all of this, we are still attached to, *If I do this, this can happen*, instead of, *We can support the best that we can support and surrender the rest*," she offers.

Sometimes when it comes to family, I wonder if my chosen and crafted-over-time beliefs have ever truly rooted. Because sometimes when I am with my family of origin, I drop into behaviors and reactions I was sure I had grown past. Or a disproportionate reaction emerges from no discernible place. "It's like you're yourself against yourself. And I wonder which one of me is right sometimes. Because if I believe what I say I believe in—how did I just abdicate myself?" I ask myself as much as I ask her.

"It's a razor's edge. It's so crazy when we talk about the veils being lifted. How we are born, the families we are born into, the environment we are born into. These are catalysts for us to evolve, to break our own insidious patterns of ignorance. The more we go in and say, *I'm in this. I'm in this to win this, I want to participate*, it's almost like the gods say: *Okay, you wanna play? Let's play*," she says. "When we relate to our family, we think, *Well if that is you, that must be me, too*. We are so deeply connected. In one way, we can talk it through, do some work and some practices. We can engage what we think will liberate us, but the work that we need to do will always rise up, and it usually comes through the ones that are closest to us," she articulates.

"It's very humbling. There is so much work we can do with what is very close to us in our own ecosystem, our own sphere. *So, okay*, I say. I will be quiet and still and see what is right in front of me and serve what is right in front of me," Lilavati says. "Because that is going to keep me stable. That is going to enhance the energy of muladhara, or root chakra. I'll feel more stable, more grounded, and more fortified and powerful."

I listen as she speaks the truth underneath the surface. The reality that in the brilliance, there is the muck, the contradiction. That the medicine is again not in the running away from but in the being with.

"When life smacks down, we want to get out of it right away. *When's it gonna be over? When's it gonna be over?* No, this is the beauty," she commands us into the moment. "This is where we get to the other place," she says.

"Okay, I'm going to pause you here. When you have that feeling, that *I need to get out immediately*, can you really access the beauty? If you were to go practical, is that the next step? Or is it stillness? Does beauty happen after? If you can't see the beauty, what is the thing you can do to open your eyes?"

"I think for me, it's faith. I have been introduced to so much grace in my life. I have this faith that I am here for some reason, and I—I have experienced a lot of smack downs in my life. It has not been an easy path with relationships, with my offspring, with my parents. Everything has been dynamically charged." She weighs her voice for emphasis. "And yet I am able, through these practices, I guess, to find the stillness. To be in the essence of," she exhales, "seeing this is in my life for me to see as a teaching, to guide me deeper. It all exists as beauty, even the most horrific of circumstances are provided for us to see life is the end (Shiva) and the creation (Brahma). It comes back down to being humble," Lilavati builds. "Having the gratitude for this moment no matter how horrific things get," she exhales.

The way out is through. Beauty abounds, and your humility will give you wings.

No matter what the chasm or the peak you stand upon, as Lilavati says, at "any given time, there is this mantra that has been chanted for thousands of years: *Sathyam Shivam Sundaram.* It is that when we may exist in Truth, the Universe opens up and provides us with all the tools that we need, and the end result is beauty."

Sometimes, no matter what your tools, your placement, or your connections, you cannot get yourself out of it—no matter what *it* is. It is then that Grace rains down and lifts you up. When all of those unknown steps add up to an unknown arrival, it can be through unexpected people, a moment of clarity, a surrender, or an ending to support your growth. Perhaps the realization that everything surrounding you is for you will bring the beauty to bloom.

*** This chapter was a compilation of two separate podcasts with Lilavati, 2020 and 2019, both are available on the Rebirth podcast.***

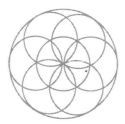

Serendipity Arrives and Tools to Greet Her

I taught high school English for five years in a suburb that met the edge of the Philadelphia school district. I am slight of build and complexion. That means I had to show my lanyard of identification to get into the teacher's lounge because at 27, they thought I was a student. My slight stature didn't bode well for me with my first-year students. Basically, I was their catnip.

"How did you learn that?" one of my students in one of my most intimidating classes asked. Teaching until you get your sea legs can be a scary thing. I was teaching sophomores during third period, in a class that had an alchemy of high intelligence on a bumpy road.

The girl that had interrupted me was 16, but her eyes also told me that she held earned wisdom.

"Well," I answered her even though she had cut off my lecture mid-sentence, "I taught car dealers how to communicate with their staff, and I learned—"

"I thought you said you helped kids with their tests, and that's where your big vocabulary came from."

"Yes, I did that. I also learned some of these things you were asking me about when I was a waitress—"

"You ain't old enough to have done all these things," the 16-year-old informed me.

But I was. I have had many jobs and experiences that have been born of listening to life's promptings. Teaching, however, was the only career where at my first six-month review, I told my boss I couldn't do it.

"What do you mean?" he asked, seated at his rectangular metal desk.

I proceeded to be more honest than I was ever taught to be. I told him that I thought I was failing. That the kids were running ahead of me and that I was not meeting their needs. I confided in him that I was not an equipped teacher and that I was intimidated by my third period class.

What he said next shocked me more than my honesty. He told me I had just proven to him how much I cared and therefore what a good teacher I would become, and that no one got the grasp of teaching in their first year. In fact, he counseled, it would most likely not be until my second or third year that I would know what kind of teacher I was. He said that he had seen how much I was invested and trying, and to not underestimate what the students gained from my dedication and first-year exuberance.

I was shocked. I had been so used to excelling that I didn't understand I was in a career that could only be learned by doing. That man's name is Rick Topper, and I am so grateful that he chose to nurture me because teaching became, and still is, one of my greatest passions and joys.

Serendipity is something to expect, yet it cannot be controlled or predicted. It is an aligned magic that is reflective of how life is wanting to flow for and through you. Sometimes, you may be working with your tools, chipping away at a goal, maintaining a focus, and this gentle breeze moves through the room and something bigger than the sum of your actions and better than you could have orchestrated arrives. That was the synchronistic whisper that birthed Rebirth the podcast into a book. Remember when I said that if you keep at it, what you think you cannot achieve may deliver the medicine you need? That is what happened with Rebirth. And it is how life works—when we are available for it.

Meet Martina Faulkner

I met Martina Faulkner over a decade ago in a cranial-sacral retreat on Maui. My initial visits to Maui assisting with retreats helped me soften the rather unnavigated straight lines of my childhood of how things worked. I began to understand with my own eyes… Actually, life took me by the hand and said, *I'm going to need you to open up your perspective to do the work you are here to do.* Being a teaching assistant on a half-dozen cranial-sacral retreats while I was still an English teacher availed me to a whole other world of healing and learning. People came together to lay down burdens, learn healing modalities, and open up to interconnected perspectives on living. I saw with my own eyes that life was indeed magic, that healing happened. Nature was boundless, and people, so many people, had so many gifts. Martina Faulkner was one of those gifted people I met on Maui, guided by her commitment to living fully.

"One of the things I appreciate about you, Martina," I begin, "is that you have gifts of the business world and also of the spiritual world. That although they are innate, you have made the choice and the practice to develop them."

"I love the choice of your word *develop*," Martina affirms. She tells us that around two decades ago, she felt life tapping at her shoulder, which she evaded while she was happily ensconced in her familiar corporate life.

> "The Universe lovingly let me run away, would come back and tap me on the shoulder with something new. Then circle back around and tap me again on the shoulder—Here, look at this. Until eventually I had no choice but to turn around and say, *Okay, what do you want?* Once I did that, then everything started to flow," Martina says.

I laugh. "I think some people right now might be confused and think—*Wait, this is a publisher?* But that is why I wanted you to be on the show. The rules are breaking, blending, and dismantling. Can you talk to us about what you are bringing to the world now?" I ask.

"I feel like I am a midwife to the creation of new work in the world. I am not the one birthing it; I created the situation—or platform, if you will—in which other people can give birth, which is Inspirebytes Omni Media. As we see around us, there are a lot of things happening that are inviting us, if not in some cases pushing us, to just expand our vision a little bit into the peripheral vision that we have somewhat ignored and allow that to be part of the whole picture.

"The idea came six years ago when I was on my own journey with my first book. I got a contract with a publisher, and I was flummoxed that anybody would sign a contract like that because it was so not author-friendly. I did my due diligence, checked in with some people I know in publishing in New York, and they were like, *Yeah, I wouldn't sign that.* So I started researching—what is going on in the publishing world? What is the publishing world? Every time I dug something up, a voice inside me said, *There has to be a better way; there has to be another way.* I kept looking for another way, which planted a seed six years ago that *Maybe I should create the other way.* Then life happened, and I self-published my first book. But all the while this seed was germinating and growing roots.

"Then two years ago, the roots took hold and the other way came forth. So now I get to be the person who invites people into the other way to share their voice and work with the world. I think one of my gifts," Martina shares proudly, "is I see potential, and I genuinely feel that I know how to invite someone into their potential. This is part of my work as life coach, therapist, healer, intuitive—but it is also part of my work as a publisher. Most of the people in the company are there because I saw potential and I made a phone call. I said, 'I think you have something here. Would you allow me to help you bring it forth?'"

I remember answering her call when I had just parallel parked my car. I answered spontaneously, a little surprised to see her name.

"You're what? And yes, I am interested," were my unfettered responses. Part of me was clear that if you wanted to write and someone you know calls you and says they want to publish you, you say yes.

At the time, I only had a little thing written. I mean, I talked about writing a lot. I had fits and starts in scads of notebooks and oodles of projects sitting in Word documents, never seen. I taught English for 10 years. I climbed trees to read books as a child. I have kept a journal my whole life, including my first one at six where I chronicled a life of cartoons and siblings. It had Lucy from Peanuts on the front yelling, *Stay Out!*, and it had a lock. I loved writing. My whole life, people said I would write a book. I thought it would be great—someday. You know, when I was ready.

But here I was, my small babe asleep in his car seat, standing on a busy side street, listening to this woman talk to me about lawyers and founders and mission statements and talent and wanting to select voices that would make a difference, and she knew my writing would.

"Would you like to be one of our authors, Kate?" Her voice pierced through to the present moment.

I remember looking at my sleeping child in his car seat and then looking up to a corner in my mind, a place where I go to check in with myself, and I heard myself say: "Yes, of course."

I told no one.

I sat with the reality and the fantasy that this conversation might have actually happened. The mini-book, as I had referred to it, was called *Start Now, Love*. A guidebook to birthing your passions and staying on the creative path as inspired by being self-employed and in the healing arts myself. It is not, by the way, the book that got published.

I signed a contract, and nothing came creatively. I mean nothing. I know the nothing of germination, and I know the nothing of: *Nope, nothing to see here*. Every time I tried to add more to that initial book, it felt forced. There was no spark. I was more than a little stuck. This had happened when I was in a writing workshop with Cheryl Strayed, and my writing was so bad—I mean so bad—she did not even critique it. Rather, she offered kind support for me to find my voice, which is a kiss of death, for a writer, to be treated with kid gloves rather than withstanding the criticism of a professional.

I actually stopped writing for a year after that. For the first time in my life, I put the pen down. Then, one day a little over a year later, out of nowhere, the Muse walked back into my life, cleared her throat, and tapped the table. *Write*, she said.

I did; my writing voice had changed.

Without mentioning that I was sitting amidst the deafening roar of writer's block, I invited Martina to share her inspiration and evolution in publishing on my podcast.

If there is doubt in your mind, take pause in your actions.

The day after the podcast is released, Martina calls and says: "I listened to the podcast. Let's make Rebirth the book." I felt the lightning of clarity in her idea. The rush of inspiration began, and here we are. You and me, sharing stories together.

The road that leads us to where we are going can dip and turn and even at times disappear in the fog, forcing us to pull over, to pause. Martina talks about that as she shares the thread of her own life and work.

"Can you talk about when doubt shows up and what role it plays?" I ask

"Certainly. Doubt shows up for everyone, and I think if you say you are without doubt, then you have denial."

We both chuckle.

"There are a few things that I have written over the years that stand out to me. One of them is, *If there is doubt in your mind, take pause in your actions.* I think doubt is the invitation into the pause. As a theater major, I learned you need a pause to have a shift in the action, in order to have a shift in the intention, in order to have a shift in the plotline.

"The Pause is one of the most critical moments in our progression. The Pause allows us to reevaluate, to double down, to take a breath so that you have energy to keep going. So the doubt, to me, is an invitation to pause. It allows us to say:

1. Do I really want this?
2. Do I want it differently?
3. What am I missing while I am plowing through? Again, time to expand peripheral vision.

"When you align with doubt rather than fear it, it can become an incredibly powerful tool in your life. There was no way I was going to create a company and not experience doubt. I still experience doubt."

"I think it is helpful to mention that we can have a skillset in one area that doesn't exactly translate to another, so we can be moving along and the doubt pops up in an unexpected place," I add. Maybe you are more organized in the kitchen than your office. Or you excel at work scheduling, but drop off some of your own event management (like down time!). Or maybe you know one day that you have clarity on where you are going, and the next morning you wake up questioning yourself all over again.

"Now, you're not always going to come out of doubt, click your heels, and you are off to Oz. There are times when doubt, for me at least, would linger," Martina shares. "I would wake up in the morning and think, *All these beautiful authors and talent are trusting me, and they really shouldn't*. I have absolute doubt that I can do right by them because I hold their beauty in my hands. I have asked them to bring forth their beauty, and they are trusting me to steward it, to midwife it, and there have been days when I am genuinely not sure I know what I am doing.

"Those are days that I have learned—over time, because it is a muscle you have to flex—to call a friend. Call a trusted, vetted person, and tell them, 'I am swimming upstream.' And that person is going to say, 'That's okay.' And it doesn't have to have an explanation. It can just be okay. It is usually enough for me to be back at it a day later."

"Vetted is a great word," I say.

"They have to be vetted, because," Martina's voice goes up, "I have certainly called people who are not vetted, and they have been like, 'Yeah, I don't know why you chose to do this.' And I've been like, *Well that is not helpful*."

I have done that, too. That's how we learn to trust ourselves and the preciousness of our dreams, by knowing who to trust them with, especially in their infancy.

"So really," I ask Martina. "How do you start a publishing and media company? You're dialing phone calls to make a dream come true? Sometimes when people talk about spirituality, one of the reasons it gets dismissed [is] because it seems that the choices are to hang out in the ethers or be super grounded, but I think it is the marriage of the two."

"It's the marriage of the two," she confirms. "We are not a soul having a human experience or a human with a soul; we are 'both and.' And when you lean in, to borrow a phrase from another woman, to that 'both and' proposition of being human *and* soul, you allow for greater potential. When I lean in and remember that—for me, things happen. Things happen that I didn't even have to make happen. You have to show up for it, of course."

"Can you give us an example of showing up for it?" I pinpoint.

"I do something called bookending. You have a problem, and you put it in the middle, and you approach it from two sides. Those two sides are the human side and the divine side. You cut the time it takes to get to the solution in half because you are coming at it from two sides. When I lean into [the] being human [side], it means I have learned to compartmentalize being 100% human, putting my corporate hat back on, running numbers, looking at spreadsheets, and making decisions. I literally have a note on my computer that simply says: 'You're the boss, make decisions and move on.'"

"Thank you. So let's pause for a minute and go into your corporate background to orient us," I direct.

"Before I became an entrepreneur and a writer," Martina says, "I was a buyer for Neiman Marcus. Before that, I was in sales and apartment leasing. Before that, I was a stylist. Before that, I worked as a fundraiser for a major medical school. Before that, I worked in business consulting. Before that, I worked in program development. And when I first graduated college, I was a paraprofessional in a legal firm. So I have had my toe in a lot of different businesses."

"Each a chapter in a book to water [a] germinating seed," I say, happily mixing metaphors.

"Exactly," she laughs.

You don't leave behind the things you learn; you pull knowledge from one world and apply it to the next. It may actually be how life is working you and growing you towards your next evolution. Martina reflected that in her wide and various roles, the through line was relationship building.

"Which is exactly what I put into all that I do today, especially when I go into the divine side, especially when I go into the spiritual side to use those gifts."

I add, "Sometimes when people leave a traditional job, they think they need to leave everything else, but you don't leave those excel spreadsheets behind. It comes with you if you want to build something in form."

"It has to come with [you] because it is part of you. There are no mistakes in your journey," Martina shares. "So if you learn something in an accounting firm, and go have a breakthrough and become a yoga teacher, you want to open a yoga studio. What you learned in the accounting firm should be brought with you. It was part of your journey for a reason. Whether it was learning spreadsheets or learning how to say no to an unnecessary request from a boss or learning how to manage other people, or, or, or. We all learn different things for a reason, and they are cumulative for a reason.

"I can see it now, now that I am putting it all into play, even including my degree in drama," Martina chuckles. "I am so grateful for this crazy, snaking, meandering path that I had that a lot of traditional people scoffed at. But look at what I can do, look at who I can talk to, look at what I can manifest, and create, and help others create because I had all of these random and corporate-type experiences."

"Listening to your story, there has to be a cultivation of listening to yourself," I clarify. "Which sounds obvious... "

"I'm not 100% sure it is obvious. I think it is obvious if you have been knocked to your butt enough times, and you look around and go, *I'm down here by myself, I best start listening to me*. I don't think it is inherently obvious that we should listen to ourselves. There are a couple of reasons for that, in my opinion. One, we're women. We will listen to others as long as the day is long. We are hardwired to do that... We are also societally wired to discount and discredit our own selves and our voices, for decades upon decades. When I tell my clients to pause and look at the programming you have passively received for decades, don't beat yourself up. There's a reason why you think the way you think— we just have to help you remember who you are so you can think differently."

"And if you let shame stay for too long, it will block the progress," I add.

"Absolutely. Shame is one of those things when you start to understand how it plays a role in your life, you can start to make different choices around how you show up for yourself. I am actually trained and certified in Brené Brown's work with shame and resilience. I don't think shame ever goes away. But I do think resilience can build so strongly that shame then becomes a moment as opposed to a perpetual movement through your life.

"Back to listening to yourself—[it's] not so obvious," Martina orients us. "I think also there is this notion of intuition. Everybody has it. Intuition is like a volume dial. You are either at a zero or a ten, and most people are somewhere in between. Working with your intuition and fine-tuning it, learning how to work that dial, you can turn the volume up and down. I could walk around with my intuition volume on nine all day, but that is exhausting... and not human. So I walk around daily, let's say with a five, and then when I am working with clients or getting quiet within myself, I turn the volume up. We can all learn to do that. Intuition is one of these things that has to do with listening—listening to yourself, listening to the Universe—that I think we all have. But let's go back to your word: develop. We have to develop the skill set to move that volume control knob."

"Would you say that dials back to the other end of bookending?"

> "I do. When I see somebody who has potential, that is a human thing and a soul thing. I have to feel into [it]. *Am I really recognizing this potential, or am I starry-eyed? Is there really something here that is marketable and saleable?* Then I go back to the starry-eyed side, and I ask myself, *How do I feel when I am around this person's work? What [does] my intuition tell me about this person's work?* Because here is the other truth: I could invite somebody, show up all day long, and I can make a platform, but if *they* don't feel good about their own work, it doesn't matter. You cannot make someone drink even if they are dying of thirst. That is part of respecting their journey, and that is very much the spiritual side."

I have to bring you behind the scenes at this moment, friend. On my last day of writing for my first draft, I was writing this chapter. I woke up refreshed in the morning and peered out the window to see the most luscious mist at 6 am on a July morning. I knew today was the day to let this book go. That's what happens when you finish something. It is no longer invisible—it takes up its own space in the world. It's released to its own life. Yes, there would be rounds of editing and such to come, but this one morning was when I went from *writing a book someday* to *I have written a book draft today*.

I made a cup of beautiful coffee, twirled up my hair, and plugged away. A good two hours in, my faithful companion, Ahonui, my black dog with one white paw, started prancing around the kitchen for my attention.

"Not now," I told her, letting her out and in, out and in the backyard. She left for a nap. Then returned an hour later, click-clacking across the kitchen floor.

I looked at her perked ears and knowing eyes. I had been going at a great clip, on track for my noon deadline, and I was writing Martina's segment about an author feeling good about their work, and my computer froze. Full on froze.

I didn't feel panic. I looked at Nui, then back at the computer, and surrendered. I walked out of the house disheveled with a baseball cap that read, *Live Happy*. It was gloriously perfect outside with blue skies and a cool, shining sun. *I'm birthing my book today*, I actually allowed myself to realize for the first time.

I looked at the black blur of a dog running carefree across the open field. I looked at the shining sun. *I am birthing my book today*. I thought of all the serendipities. All the false starts and stops. The times I thought I would have to break the contract. The times that I diminished the worthwhileness of the book, only to be toppled over, similar to what Martina shared. To be holding all of these stories, to be entrusted to share them. Everyone I asked, who had been on the podcast, if I could share their story in a book, not only said yes but congratulated me, and I had not stopped to truly appreciate all the little moments that brought me here. The meeting of these individuals, the traversing of doubt and hard times, the making the commitment to show up and sit and write, the worthwhileness of the work itself. All that and more were wrapped up into this one moment that a knowing dog and sensitive computer got me to slow me down and be present to the moment.

Martina continues, "You have to believe the space you take up on this planet is valid."

When we accept that space, it can fill with delicious and magical things. A great example is the route that Martina's second book took to birthing. In August of 2019, Martina was looking for an illustrator for one of her authors in the company.

> "I happened to find Kelly Ulrich on IG and sent some of her images to my author, who said the images were lovely and had the feeling we want," Martina explains.

> "So I reached out to this total stranger [and] told her I started this publishing company. And at the time, I had myself and this other author as an author. That's it. Two authors in the company—

talk about taking a leap of faith. So she and I had a conversation, Kelly did a preliminary illustration—the author loved it, so I signed Kelly immediately. Then I come to find out she had also written children's books, so I signed her for those, and they will come out over the next five to ten years because there are many of them."

Kelly and Martina were working on their wonderful relationship as illustrator and publisher when the world took a new course in 2020. Through their professional relationship and kindred conversations, they decided to create a book to help the children through these confusing times. The next day, an ultimately untrue fantasy about the dolphins returning to the canals of Venice inspired Martina to look for other natural phenomena happening throughout the world. She found many and pitched an idea to Kelly, who loved it. Martina compiled a list of all the animal stories she had found. When inspiration aligned, she wrote the text of the book in an hour. Martina points out this is one of those "both and" moments. The book birthed quickly since she already had organized her research, *and* she held a clear understanding of how a children's book needs to work.

There is the energy of striving for completion and space-setting for inspiration. It takes both.

> "When I sent it to Kelly, she was already seeing the paintings," Martina recalls. "And this is the premise behind the company: Collaboration matters. Collaboration is part of the new paradigm. It is not a 'me vs. you' or 'us vs. them.' 'All the money for me, not for you.' It's about what we can do together to make things better and provide for ourselves along the way."

Hearing her say this reminded me of Stephanie Cohen sharing her evolution with Mompops popsicles. It was another way to make a difference in which everyone was being served.

> Martina expands, "I don't believe in the whole 'starving artist' thing. It is something we bought into because the paradigm

wanted us to. I want all my artists and my authors to make money, and I want the company to make money because the more money we make, the more authors we can sign. It's that simple. It's flow. It's about possibility and flow.

"So this book comes out, Kate," Martina adds, "and I stopped and I realized we wrote a book about conservation without intending to write a book about conservation. [*When the World Went Quiet*] took on a whole new life of its own; we got this award-winning conservation photographer to endorse the book, and it has become this beautiful remembrance of a really difficult time, and the reviews of the parents sharing what the kids are saying—my heart could not be happier.

"When I created the company, I was—and am—very adamant about values and tenets. The tenets of the company are: service, authenticity, integrity, and fun. I have learned over the years, if it is not fun, people are not learning as well as they could be and not showing up as much as they would be. You have to have that element of fun."

I think holding the space for fun is more necessary than we realize, and that's what my dog was reminding me that morning in the field. Don't rush past the moment. Have fun. Soak it up. Make space for possibilities and integration.

Martina talks about this perspective shift in her first book, *What if..?*

Before writing the book, while working with her coaching clients, she explains, "I kept hearing clients say: What if I get sick? What if I lose my job? What if he doesn't like me? What if she this? Or that? Everything was externalized to their being.

"My response would not be to negate their experience. My response would be, *Let me invite you to experience something different.* So I would say: 'What if the reverse is true? What's possible?' And it took my clients out of the energy of *nothing's possible*, into the energy of *I have permission to daydream?*"

"It's as simple as that." I nod my head.

> "It really is. It really, really is," Martina affirms. "We come back to, *We have to pause to pivot.* We have this shift from *What if my life is a disaster?* to *What if I have a say in my life? Now what can we do?* And that's when my mentor José Stevens said, 'Write the book already.' So I did."

And that is the book that planted the seed, that watered the thought, that birthed the company whose publisher called to invite an author who wrote the book, born of serendipity, that sits in your hand today.

Whatever you are here to birth is a creative act, and it needs you as much as you need it. It is tied up in your liberation, or it wouldn't be hanging around.

As Steven Pressfield reminds us, "The mother and the artist are watched over by heaven. Nature's wisdom knows when it's time for the life within to switch from gills to lungs. It knows down to the nanosecond when the first tiny fingernails may appear... Let's ask ourselves like that new mother: What do I feel growing inside of me? Let me bring that forth, if I can" (157).

Your desires, to borrow a phrase from another woman, are holy. Your journey is now; it is yours for the claiming. So when the call comes, answer it.

As mentioned, the phrases borrowed from other women in this chapter are: "Lean in" by Sheryl Sandberg and "Your desires are holy" by Amanda Frances

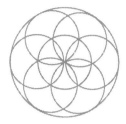

Remember Who You Are

We often end where we begin. We look back and it all makes sense. Our sight and our fortitude can't be honed by simulation. It takes the alchemy of grit and doubt fused into fortitude by the beating of our heart and the choice to keep going. It's as simple and as difficult as that.

Joe Longo is a manifestation coach. He wasn't always one. He was married to a woman that brought the art of yoga into his life, yet it wasn't until they were divorced that he walked away from his IT job, walked more deeply into a structure of spiritual inquiry, and it would be another 10 years until he was sitting in the space that was germinating for him in doing all of what he loved in a form that was his highest service—to himself and others. Did I mention he was my neighbor in my twenties? That his wife also introduced me to David Newman and Yoga on Main? That I was in their wedding, and divorce didn't stop any of the aforementioned friendships?

I remember going on a short hike on a brisk day with him almost two years ago when he asked what I thought about his enrolling in a coaching program. The cost would have been one that would make him slightly uneasy. That is always a sign of growth—slight unease, a quiver in the expansion. When it comes to others, Joe, a natural intuitive, has a really great way of seeing and supporting where others would shine in their own lives. Phenomenal qualities in a coach, and in a friend.

A year before that, he interviewed me on his 30 Days of Inspiration, a creative project he did to commit to creating content and growing his business doing what he loved. Our episode got a good viewing. Joe called a few weeks later and said that "a podcast might be a good idea for you." He showed up with a microphone, a tutorial, and editing support. Rebirth was born. But let's go back to our short hike and the moment before Joe started on this new and clearly destined path.

I reminded him of his hand in birthing my podcast on our walk that day as he was on the precipice of his own new decision, "Joe," I said, "a year after your suggestion, I am starting Season 2 of Rebirth, and I love it more than I expected. Where do you want to be a year later?"

I can tell you where he ended up a year later: He was a featured speaker on the coaching program platform that he successfully graduated from. A lot can happen in a year when we are aligned. A year can float by unnoticed if we are lost. Joe reminds us it is all part of the process of becoming who we already are.

We think we need to make the things happen. But like Lilavati hints, this may not be so. Rather than pushing the river, we may best be served by putting forth what is being asked of us, then (here's the kicker) surrendering to the how and the when and being ready when that perfect moment, that perfect match for you and your vision arrives. The clues are there all along; our work is to be present to them.

Meet Joe Longo

"Can we talk," I ask, "about how there was no prep for this call?"

"None at all," Joe laughs.

"We tried a few times," I offer.

"A few times. Never worked. Big no." He laughs some more.

"Then I sent you an invitation without warning, and you were there. With no heads up. And we are recording."

"Yup," Joe says.

"So when we say do the work, be ready, because you never know when the call is going to come—this podcast is literal proof of that."

"Yes," Joe exhales. "Be present."

Over the past 10 years, Joe has been leading Manifestation workshops using Kundalini Yoga as a starting point to get people motivated. Then he shares techniques that have worked for himself, clients, and friends. Through that decade, Joe also maintained his photography business, eventually letting the art of photography support the calling of life coach. It was a journey—not an instant manifestation.

> "As I teach manifestation, we all want instant gratification—our phone gives it to us. We want that blast of dopamine. So for manifesting, we want it to happen quick. *But* if we're not ready..." his trailing off voice insinuates before he doubles back with a laugh. "Because I am literally experiencing this right now," Joe chuckles in honesty. "Because I think I asked for all of this nine years ago and NOW it's showing up."

"Yeah, well." I laugh and add, "Is it showing up, or are *you* showing up?"

"Well, there you go exactly," Joe agrees. "I'm now ready to receive what I asked for so long ago. And literally it's like I forgot I asked for it."

"I had a similar realization recently, sifting through old journals," I add. "And seeing that I had written the same lists, same clarity, same desires—for years." Honestly friend, it was at first embarrassing to read, re-read, and read again, journal after journal of the lists of intentions and unwindings of things I could not understand, shake, or let go. So I was a little over-enthused when Joe mentioned this very same realization.

> "Yes!" he replies. "On Jessa Reed's podcast, OD, she talks about this. We focus on what we don't want. Imagine being at a restaurant and the waiter comes up for your order and all you say is what you don't want:
>
> 'I don't want the crabcakes,' you say.
>
> 'Cool, tell me what you *do want*,' the waiter counters.
>
> 'I don't want the crabcakes,' you repeat."

I cracked up. Do you do this? *I* do this. I do this so much that it became a conscious practice of mine to *undo* this habit. It is the quickest way to stay stuck, to not allow yourself to lean into what could be, to focus on your definite no. It's the same permission Martina gave us, to daydream. Still chuckling, I offer, "This is the best metaphor I've heard, Joe."

> "Right? And then Jessa went on to say that some manifestations do not take a day, and sometimes it takes years. Wow," he laughs contagiously, "some of this has taken a long time. As I am sitting with these things and looking back, I can see: *Oh, right. That is where I got in my own way.*"

Oftentimes when I talk with Joe, we laugh about how we unknowingly can track similar revelations. This was one of those moments; there is something so fun about confirmation *after the fact*. You get the empowerment of the discovery and the joy of knowing you are not alone. I tell him, "I recently was doing automatic writing on why my most recent partnership ended in dissolution. I was asking, *Why did it have to happen that way? Why did I have to choose that environment to say I wanted to learn a lesson?*"

Let me slow this down, because I think it is important. I had the intention to learn a lesson. I assumed that I would succeed. Succeeding and learning are not one and the same in the school of life. Remember how long it took

Martina for her seed to grow roots? Was that a failure? No, it was a learning. Me, with my killer book covers, had always linked learning with straight A's and straight lines. However, sometimes that unwinding is so deep, and that learning is so wide, that first it is felt only on the inside before it can reflect out, sturdy enough to withstand the world.

It is in our missteps that we truly learn.

I attempt to articulate this to Joe. "It was as if life said to me, 'Okay, Kate, I hear you. It looks like first you need to fail so you are willing to learn.'"

"Right, but I think sometimes failures sound harsh," Joe counters. "It is in those failures or missteps that we truly learn: 'Oh right, that is what I needed to learn from this. I needed to go down this path for the things that are now showing up. I needed to walk the path I was walking until I got to where I am now—ready.'"

"Totally," I agree.

"I started watching *Silicon Valley* again—very funny—but there [was] this underlying theme," Joe extends. "That you just keep failing and failing and you keep practicing and tweaking, asking for help when help is needed. It's so relevant in life."

I know Joe was talking about a sitcom, but a friend of mine who worked in Silicon Valley helped make failure a part of my lexicon. He said: "Kate, you have to learn how to fail."

I told him, "I don't fail." To which he answered very much like Stephanie Cohen did: *"Kate that's your problem; everyone fails. If you don't learn how to fail, you're not actually growing."* If I am honest, my interior dialogue was rattled—because my first ingrained response is that you have to do everything well. I learned—am learning—that right and well has a time, but failing and learning to grow a new way has a season, too.

"This may be a little controversial," Joe responds. "But this is the main reason that I think participation trophies for children are not a good idea. You have to lose. Growing up, the biggest lessons that I learned that taught me to be okay with life were losing. I lost a lot!

"The teams I was on weren't good. We always lost. But every time we lost, I realized there were more important things than this game. In 11th grade, my football team won one game. It wasn't even a good game... When you continually lose, week after week after week, when you have 15 weeks of this—you learn a lot. That really shaped me as a young man. You gotta keep going," he laughs in all sincerity. "Then you move into that space later on of letting go and allowing." Joe ties this to his client work now. "I started telling my clients, 'This isn't going to happen overnight. You have to put the work in.'"

"I hear you using the term remembering. I would love to hear you talk about that," I offer.

"Would love to. We're not awakening. We're awake. We woke up. We just don't remember. It's like that soul contract. We signed a soul contract to come to this spinning rock, and we promised to forget everything we have ever learned about every time we have ever been here so we could keep growing and learning. I started thinking about my life and how many times throughout my life I had a glimpse of remembering. Remembering my essence, remembering that I was more than I thought I was. Does that make sense?"

"Yes," I say.

"I am connected to everything. And then I forget. I think it is just part of our human nature to forget because it's too much for us to grasp all at once. So we get a little glimpse and then we forget—and then something else," Joe snaps his fingers, "makes us remember. It depends on your wave of awareness."

"I love adding the reminder of frequency," I share. "We meet people in our lives that are always in a good mood and do not necessarily hide their difficulties, yet do their best to focus on the positive with effort. I think remembering and choosing to cultivate frequency opens the bandwidth of remembering, as you say. I am beginning to believe more and more in Rumi's quote to not 'seek love but seek to remove all the barriers to it.' I used to think it was so cheesy. Now I think it is true."

"So true," Joe says. "I think ultimately, it comes down to awareness," Joe grounds the conversation. "Where are you in your own self-awareness? Then start noticing the things that put you in a lower vibrational state or a higher vibrational state. See if you can catch it, 'Oh, wait a minute, if I go down this road, it's not going to take me where I want to go, so you decide to turn.' It is a fine balance. The awareness and the balance. It's what it is all about," he says.

Martina talks about remembering we are both human and divine. Lilavati told us the whole cosmos is within us. We are powerful and we are fragile. We can be swept up in grace, and we can receive the culmination of all our choices. It is all true. In addition to his positive attitude, Joe does a great job of making those small choices that open up into new opportunities in his own work and supporting others.

"You are the reason this podcast exists," I tell him.

"Oh stop, you're the reason the podcast exists," Joe volleys right back. Although this is true, so is the power of frequency and vibration and how we are not designed to go it alone. How sometimes we push, sometimes we pull. Sometimes we carry others, and sometimes we are carried.

"No, no. It's okay." I smile. "I think this is a powerful example of how you do not need to know the how, but you do need to cultivate a vibration of that which you want to bring into your life. If you had not been like: 'Hey, Kate, I think you'd really enjoy a podcast...' all of this might not have happened. When you suggested it, I thought, *Yeah, I don't think I can do that.*"

I continue recounting to Joe, "But you were like: 'Nah, actually you could, and we're gonna help set you up, and it's gonna be really fun.'"

It ends up being true—"Here we are in Season 4!" I cheer. "And the show then went on to its own rebirth, its own growth. Watching how all that is happening is part of the reason I wanted to have you back on the show—a full circle fruition. I would never have picked a podcast—but I had a frequency network around me that allowed the invitation to come in a way that I would not have known myself. That's okay. You don't have to know everything to be in alignment for it to come," I find this so hopeful and yet so easy to forget.

"Right," Joe confirms, "and I think that circles back to the level of awareness and the being ready to receive the signs that are coming at us."

"Especially when people are saying, *I can't trust anything. I don't know anything,*" I respond, "Well actually, because of all the chaos, if you can get your eyes an inch or two above the muck, there is a lot of clarity."

> "There's so much. And when there's so much muck... it can actually feel a little scary to sit down and actually breathe and go within and see if I can see, feel, hear anything that might be coming to me that the Universe might have to say to me," Joe illuminates.

> "The more I coach and study different coaches and theories, I keep running into the thought that a lot of us are our own obstacles, and we become our own obstacles not because we are afraid of failing, but we are afraid of succeeding. What is gonna happen if I actually make this work? That whole way of thinking is now

completely flipped on its head, and I actually get what I want, too?" says Joe incredulously.

"... I have been thinking about what makes us squash," I share. "Almost like we come in really big, and then the people around us squash us just a bit so we can fit in, so we can get a job, so we can have friends—then you get to a later part of your life, and you realize the whole real thing was to be bigger... I am wondering what we could do for less squashing." I wonder this for myself, and I wonder this for my child.

Joe shares open-heartedly, "I think we need to celebrate each other and celebrate our successes. Unfortunately, most humans would rather say: *Why is that happening for Betty and it is not happening for me? I've been doing all this work—why are they getting it? And I am not getting it.* That keeps us in that state of wanting and needing, and woe is me. But if we can instead flip it and celebrate the successes of everyone, especially someone that is working in our same exact field—celebrate their successes. Because that is going to do more energetically to allow us to get to that space as well."

"That is so beautifully said. It can be hard though," I respond.

"Oh, so hard!" Joe agrees. "And again, because we are human, we are unfortunately programmed for the negative."

"We were taught tremendous scarcity," I add. "That there was only so much, and that is a flat out lie. It is a constructed lie. The first thing we have to understand is, what does nature tell you? Nature tells you that there is enough for everyone."

"Right, exactly. And if we look at all the great teachers throughout all of time—they say that."

"Repeatedly."

"All of them," Joe adds.

"Yet we willingly have accepted a construct that tells us otherwise, and in most cases, it probably got in without us knowing. But the great news is we can release it and choose not to impart it onward," I share.

> "The releasing of it doesn't have to be hard," Joe says with so much support. "It doesn't have to be hard. You don't have to be a wizard. You just have to believe. Literally, believe.

> "I have been saying this often," Joe continues. "I know the words are easy to say. I know it is easy for you and I to sit here and say, *Just believe it and everything will be okay.* That is not what I am saying; to truly feel and believe is work. You have to do the work in the internal space of going from *woe is me* to celebrating and really feeling. I am *not saying* just blink your eyes and feel," he laughs. "But to *really* feel it and believe is the key to all of it."

When we are the furthest from ourselves, it is the hardest to believe. Consciously or subconsciously, the muck is blocking us from the light, but the light is still there. The grace is still there, as David reminded us. The sun still shines. You are still deserving of all the things you have desired that come from *that* place. You know the one. The one that can be silly or ostentatious, maybe even make you think you are crazy! Those are the ideas that will grow you. Those are the ideas that lead you to your learning and back to who you truly are at the same time. If we are here, if we are breathing, we can be loving and learning.

When all of that feels too much, we can remember, as Joe says, that on this spinning rock, we always have that choice to tune in and turn up our vibration. Friend, when you least expect it—believe me if you don't have that belief for yourself at this moment—I promise you, grace comes.

Keep turning towards what feels good. Write those goals again and again. Call the vetted friend when the way becomes clouded. It may not come how you predicted. It may come after lessons that cause confusion or pain. It may come in a journey that takes you so far away, or one that never lets you leave and holds you in doubt so long that you cannot fathom the way out. Then one day, you surrender. The light finds a crack, and you see it all a bit differently. Or you say as Lisa O'Rear did: This life is for me, and I celebrate it exactly as it is.

Let go of the idea that you need to understand everything and step into the spiral of possibility. Cultivate your frequency—train your mind to believe it. Make friends with your power. Add heavy doses of gratitude and be ready for what calls you forward. No one else births you. No one else needs to. Remember who you are.

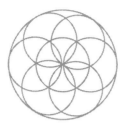

P.S.

I believe in the beauty of all things common.
I believe in the beauty of broken things.
–Terry Tempest Williams

The cosmos works by harmony of tensions, like the lyre and bow.
–Heraclitus

Somewhere around David Newman's chapter, I realized this book that was created as a resource for others was serving as a mosaiced memoir of my own rebirth. A placing of shards, of stories and journeys, of questions and tools, of triumph and resurrection, of service and doubt—all placed alongside each other, dancing in the light of lines and spirals. You cannot separate brokenness from brilliance. You cannot have leaps without falls. Life is not linear; it's a spiral of opposites in Nature's magnificent design. We return, again and again, to our magnificence that never left. As David reminded us, "It's always there. You were just somewhere else."

We are not separate from what we create—a cause for celebration and responsibility. There is not a future moment when we merge with who we are as a lost, found, or achieved thing. There is only the now moment to merge. You let go of the fight. You silence the stories that no longer serve and open to what is.

The great sage, Ramana Maharishi, says: "We imagine that we will realize the self sometime, whereas we are never anything but the self."

My lomilomi teacher, Uncle Alva, said it similarly: "One day you will wake up and trip over yourself."

Why do we hide from our greatness? Why does a baby at once burst towards life and fear the delivery? I've spent so much of my life pursuing answers—I am finally ready to settle into the inevitability of the questions, the polarity of responses, and the pristine clarity found in the light of a beautiful day that shines the undeniable truth of life's grandeur and our place in it, effortlessly and silently.

Thank you for turning around the spiral with me. May these stories serve you and those you love. May their wisdom guide you when you need it, and when it comes time, may you regale us with the turning of your own Rebirth.

With great love and gratitude,

Kate

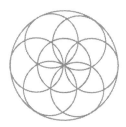

Acknowledgments

First thanks goes to the Divine Inspiration who patiently waited for me and prodded me along.

To my publisher, Martina Faulkner, for listening to the spark of knowing and picking up the phone, I am forever grateful. You paused and pushed in all the right moments. You are leading a new path for creatives. No one else would have midwifed this book as you have.

To my IOM angels: Winter Murray and Lisa Stadler, thank you for your wisdom, your guidance, and your patience in caretaking me and this book. To Claudine Wolk, for stepping forward and helping *Rebirth* find a larger space.

To my Kaua'i editors: You lovingly pulled me back and did not let me miss the moment. Thank you, Margo Orgolini, for your endless optimism and support. Thank you, Pam Woolway, for your fire and practical truth.

Myra House you captured the vision. Thank you for your beautiful and magical design work.

To Ash, at Ebru Coffee, your kindness and perfect pours helped the creative flow.

Thank you to *everyone* who has been on the Rebirth podcast, and a special thank you to the brave and supportive souls who trusted me to carry their stories on to the written page: Stephanie Cohen, thank you for being so willing and delightful. Christina Super, thank you for trusting me, supporting me, and sharing your light. Lisa O'Rear, I hope I did your story justice. Thank you for your trust. Your ferocity and tenderness are gifts. Kim Murriera, I treasure you. The wisdom and wonder you bring is medicine we all need. David Newman, thank you for sharing your gifts and your grace. Terri Simmons, my midwife and friend, you will forever hold a place of reverence and respect in my heart. Thanks for walking me through. Lilavati, I'm honored you let me put a microphone in front of you and put your words to pages. Your wisdom is needed, and your love is appreciated. Martina Faulkner, thank you for sharing your story and seeing the vision. You help others leap. Joe Longo, who knew Kingsley Street would bring my first book? Thank you for being a forever friend and an inspiration.

To my good friends who stay close, I am forever grateful for your unconditional love.

To my family, who on all sides are too numerous to name but rally behind every new adventure I go on. Thank you for supporting me—even when it doesn't make sense.

For my parents, who through their loving intuition came together a second time to lift me up. Dad, I never thought I'd be writing my first book at your dining room table, and I am grateful for it. You are a wonderful grandfather. Thank you + I love you.

Mom, you lit the flame for reading and writing to warm my life. The gifts and sacrifices are many, but it wasn't until I was much older that I understood the depth of your conviction in me not changing my major... and here we are! You moved mountains. Thank you + I love you.

My son — Little one with the big magic, I had no idea how many plans you had for us. I am running to catch up to what you already know and are teaching me, including your profound passion for excavators. You bend the world with your brightness and your laughter. You already have all that you need; remember to listen to *your* Self. Everything else will be okay.

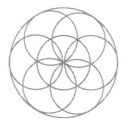

About the Author

Kate Brenton, Ed.M., educator, author, mama, and healer used to climb trees in her childhood to sit in and read books. Not much has changed, she is still inquisitive and happiest outdoors with her son and dog. A lifelong teacher, from secondary English to spiritual development, Kate has the archetype for sharing wisdom to empower and elevate.

Come say hello at www.katebrenton.com

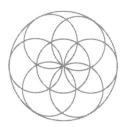

Resources

If you want to listen to the live stories of the beautiful people I speak with throughout the book, you can find them on the Rebirth podcast (https://www.katebrenton.com/rebirthpodcast) or your preferred podcast platform.

Learn more here:

Stephanie Cohen + MomPops
https://www.mompops.com

Christina Super
https://www.christinasuper.com

Lisa O'Rear
https://www.lisaorear.com

Kim Murriera
www.evolutionarybiography.com

David Newman
https://www.davidnewmanmusic.com

Terri Simmons
https://www.alchemybirthandwellness.com

Lilavati
http://www.aromabliss.com

Martina Faulkner
https://www.martinafaulkner.com
https://www.inspirebytes.com/about/

Joe Longo
https://www.inspirecreatemanifest.com

Made in the USA
Las Vegas, NV
22 September 2022

55752396R00095